S0-BRV-528

June 22, 2006

Dear Customer:

Thank you for your purchase of *Community Policing in America*, by Jeremy M. Wilson. The following information was inadvertently omitted:

This project was supported by Grant No. 2003-IJ-CX-1034 awarded by the National Institute of Justice, Office of Justice Programs, U.S. Department of Justice. Points of view in this document are those of the author and do not necessarily represent the official position or policies of the U.S. Department of Justice.

We sincerely regret any inconvenience this may have caused you. Please let us know if we can be of assistance regarding this or any other title that Taylor & Francis publishes.

Taylor & Francis Group, LLC

#RT3510X/0-415-95351-0

Community Policing
in America

Forthcoming titles in the Criminology and Justice Studies series:

*Criminal Justice Theory: Explaining the Nature and
    Behavior of Criminal Justice*
David E. Duffee and Edward R. Maguire

An Introduction to Race, Law, and American Society
Gloria Browne-Marshall

Theoretical Perspectives on Race and Crime: A Global View
Shaun L. Gabbidon

Community Policing in America

JEREMY M. WILSON

Routledge
Taylor & Francis Group
New York   London

Routledge is an imprint of the
Taylor & Francis Group, an informa business

Routledge would like to thank the Justice Research and Statistics Association for granting permission to reproduce material that originally appeared in the following journal article: Jeremy M. Wilson, "A Measurement Model Approach to Estimating Community Policing Implementation," *Justice Research and Policy 6*, no. 1 (2004): 1-24.

Published in 2006 by
Routledge
Taylor & Francis Group
270 Madison Avenue
New York, NY 10016

Published in Great Britain by
Routledge
Taylor & Francis Group
2 Park Square
Milton Park, Abingdon
Oxon OX14 4RN

Taylor & Francis Group
is the Academic Division of Informa plc.

Visit the Taylor & Francis Web site at
http://www.taylorandfrancis.com

and the Routledge Web site at
http://www.routledge-ny.com

For Angela and Alexandra,
who keep me smiling

Contents

SERIES PREFACE

Since Sir Robert Peel founded the London Metropolitan Police force in 1829, the nature and effectiveness of policing has been of interest to citizens and scholars alike. With the development of policing systems in America over the past century, various styles of policing have been implemented and their effectiveness vigorously debated. In the past few decades, however, two styles, community policing and zero-tolerance policing, have garnered particular interest among scholars. Building on the scholarly literature related to these styles of policing, Dr. Jeremy Wilson focuses on the understudied area of the implementation process of community policing. Specifically, this book examines the implementation of community policing and how various aspects of police organizations might play a role in the implementation process.

Dr. Wilson's book represents the ideal inaugural volume in the Criminology and Justice Studies series for three reasons, which clearly align with the goals set for books published in the series. First, Dr. Wilson's book focuses on an area of significance for both scholars

and criminal justice professionals. While the series will certainly pub-
lish books of relevance to either group, it is my hope that many of the
books will be of use to criminal justice professionals, who will gain
additional insights in areas that will help them make informed policy
choices. With the tremendous outlay of funds from the federal government (over $11 billion since the passage of the 1994 crime bill), the
community policing program has been in the national spotlight for
more than a decade. Such expenditures reflect the general feeling that,
by working together, the community and the police can achieve positive outcomes in crime reduction, citizen satisfaction, and the tertiary
benefit of reducing the fear of crime among citizens. Dr. Wilson's work
sheds light on the implementation of community policing in more than
four hundred jurisdictions around the country. Given the breadth and
depth of his analysis, justice professionals will certainly be interested in
the findings presented herein.

Second, this work will surely become a standard in the areas of
implementation research, organizational theory, and police organization and management. Dr. Wilson's work clearly takes these areas in
a new direction and, most importantly, pushes them to new heights.
Scholars will have to take notice of this work.

And finally, in time, I anticipate the book will become a classic in
the field, which, though lofty, represents another goal for the books
published in the series. Given the significance of the topic and the
strength of the scholarship, it is with great excitement that I present
Dr. Wilson's book as the first in the Routledge Criminology and Justice Studies Series.

Shaun L. Gabbidon, Series Editor
Criminology and Justice Studies

ACKNOWLEDGMENTS

I first would like to thank the National Institute of Justice. Their support has allowed me to continue this line of inquiry and significantly improve the model development and testing process. This book could not have been completed without the uncommon, altruistic generosity of Ed Maguire and Bill King who provided data necessary to complete the analysis and feedback throughout the research and writing process. The Community Oriented Policing Services (COPS) office also compiled data to support this project, and I am grateful to them for that.

I must also thank those who offered their generous assistance in helping me develop the intellectual and substantive framework that guided this research. Mary Marvel, Alexander Weiss, and Pamela Paxton were invaluable in this regard. The anonymous reviewers from the National Institute of Justice and Routledge also provided constructive comments, which helped to improve the research presented herein. I would like to thank Clifford Grammich and the Routledge editorial staff for their assistance in "tightening" various elements of this book. Finally, I must thank my wife, Angela, and my daughter, Alexandra, who inspire me everyday and who were patient as I developed this project.

1

INTRODUCTION

By their very nature, the police interact with the communities they
serve. The community relies upon the police to help in emergencies
and curb disorder. The police rely on the community to report crime
and provide important information that is necessary to address community concerns and solve crime. In recent decades, the scope of this
relationship has expanded. The police and community have begun to
expect more from each other as they increasingly realize they must
actively work as partners. This form of collaboration has been referred
to as community policing or community-oriented policing (COP) and
has taken many forms. The community-centered models encompass an
attempt by the police to encourage and empower the community to
become more involved in public safety, both by working with police
and dealing with problems on their own.

Significant resources have been devoted to the implementation of community policing. Since 1994, the federal Office of Community Oriented Policing Services (COPS) has given approximately $11.3 billion to local police agencies to implement COP and hire community-policing officers (COPS, 2005). The proportion of police agencies reporting they have community policing officers nearly doubled in two years, from 34 percent in 1997 to 64 percent in 1999 (Law Enforcement Management and Administrative Statistics survey data reported by Hickman and Reaves, 2001). Reported implementation is even greater in large municipal agencies with at least 100 officers; 79 percent of such agencies employed COP officers in 1997 (Bureau of Justice Statistics, 1999a).

Despite the resources expended and its proliferation, relatively little is known about the implementation of COP. There have been few statistically sensitive measures of COP implementation, the extent to which implementation varies is not certain, and the factors that facilitate or impede its implementation are not clear. The causal relationship between COP and organizational structure (e.g., what structural characteristics are most conducive to COP) has not been explored. (See Greene, 1993; Maguire, Kuhns, Uchida, and Cox, 1997; Zhao, Thurman and Lovrich, 1995.)

The scope of COP research may, ironically, contribute to the uncertainty over its implementation. Analyses of COP efforts have ranged from somewhat specific efforts such as foot patrol (e.g., Kelling et al., 1981; Trojanowicz, 1982) and crossfunctional problem-solving teams (e.g., Wilson and Donnermeyer, 2002) to concerted efforts encompassing large organizations (e.g., Skogan and Hartnett, 1997 in Chicago and Riley et al., 2005 in Cincinnati). Such analyses have demonstrated that many agencies claim to be exercising community-oriented policing while varying in their community-oriented activities and the vigor in which they implement them.

The diversity in the practice of COP raises questions on why implementation varies. With a few exceptions (e.g., Maguire et al., 1997; Zhao, 1996; Zhao, Thurman, and Lovrich, 1995), there has been little comparative analysis of COP. This research therefore seeks to identify determinants of COP implementation and how these may vary by the structure of differing police organizations.

This research is important for both practitioners and academics. It is not clear whether changes in organizational structure (e.g., for decentralized decision making and flattened hierarchies) precede COP, if COP leads police organizations to alter their structure, or if police organizational change and COP implementation are simultaneous and mutually reinforcing, with the structure of the police organization influencing the way COP is implemented and the implementation of COP leading to organizational changes. Large sample, empirical studies can help determine what factors facilitate or impede COP implementation. Such information can help police managers identify where additional planning and resources are needed.

Knowing the relative importance of the variables affecting COP implementation, including those within and beyond police control, can also help in planning community-based efforts. Such knowledge could suggest options for promoting COP in the presence of factors that inhibit it, helping stabilize COP efforts over time.

Studying COP implementation is also necessary to link implementation to outcomes. To relate COP effectiveness to its implementation, variation in its implementation must be statistically demonstrated. This work therefore develops a measure of COP implementation that can be used by practitioners, policymakers, and researchers to gauge and compare COP implementation across time and organizations. The advanced modeling techniques used to develop this measure should be of interest to academic researchers.

Academics may also be interested in this work's synthesis of organizational theory. Contingency theory suggests that the task environment of an organization (e.g., its size and age, technology, and community characteristics) determines its structure and activities. This suggests police organizations may implement COP to the extent that it assists them in managing and accomplishing their tasks. For example, police may be more inclined to implement COP if their communities are heterogeneous because it may help them better respond to the needs of diverse residents.

By contrast, institutional theory suggests the structure and activities of organizations are responses to the institutional environment. Institutional expectations of police organizations emanate from such elements as its region, funding sources, and external entities (e.g., civilian review board, union) that may exert influence over it. This suggests police organizations may implement COP to the extent it coincides with institutional expectations held by others. For example, political structures in the West tend to be more progressive (Wilson, 1968), suggesting residents of the region may expect their police organizations to be more progressive and more likely to implement innovations like COP.

These theories have often been seen as competing, but they need not be. Policing scholars have suggested both the task and institutional environments are important for understanding the functioning of police. The successful synthesis of these theories that this book attempts could therefore also be applied to analysis of factors associated with implementation of other criminal justice policies and programs.

I link both these theories to the literature on open systems and innovation, which also makes explicit the potential role that organizational structure may have in explaining COP implementation. Organizational studies have differentiated aspects of organizational structure into those pertaining to complexity and those pertaining to control. Complexity refers to differentiation in accomplishing tasks; control represents coordinating mechanisms needed to manage the complexity. From an organizational perspective, it is quite plausible that the structure of police organizations may influence the ability to implement COP. For example, organizations that are more organic in structure (e.g., informal and decentralized with flattened hierarchies) are often thought to be more innovative and therefore may be more likely to implement COP. It is also possible that structures change in response to the implementation of COP. This research examines these and other little-tested propositions of COP and its associated factors.

Though primarily written for academic researchers, this book is organized so that practitioners may selectively peruse elements most applicable to their work.

The next two chapters provide a more detailed theoretical introduction to this book. Chapter 2 defines community policing more precisely and reviews the state of implementation research, particularly its application for studying community policing. Chapter 3 reviews police organizations as open systems, and how contingency and institutional theories apply to police work. These may be of greatest interest to readers wishing for further information on the organizational theories synthesized in this book.

The subsequent three chapters describe hypothesized relationships between different elements of police organizations, community structure, and the implementation of community policing. Chapter 4 reviews organizational context and community policing. Chapter 5 reviews organizational structure and community policing. Chapter 6 reviews how elements of organizational context and may affect organizational structure. These chapters may be of greatest interest to those seeking to identify how particular elements of local police or communities may affect implementation of community policing.

The final three chapters present statistical findings on the implementation of community policing and their implications, incorporating several data sets and measures of implementation. Chapter 7 reviews the models, data, and analysis used in this research. Chapter 8 presents measurement and structural models of community policing implementation, analyzing both how widely community policing has been implemented and how it has affected police organization structure, or, conversely, how police organization structure has affected it. Chapter 9 discusses the findings and their implications.

The appendixes provide important information for those interested in using the models developed herein or their estimates. Appendix A summarizes the technical process behind structural equation modeling, and may be more interesting to researchers. However, Appendixes B and C may be of value to researchers and practitioners alike. Appendix B outlines a simple two-step process by which others can estimate community policing implementation based on the model developed in this book. Appendix C offers the model-determined estimates of community policing implementation in 1997 and 1999 for each of the sample police organizations studied in this book.

2

DEFINING COMMUNITY POLICING AND RESEARCHING ITS IMPLEMENTATION

Defining Community Policing

Community policing models have their roots in the failure of previous models of professional or reform policing to address community concerns. Despite resistance from some law enforcement circles (Zhao, Thurman, and Lovrich, 1995) and a belief that it is a passing fad (Weisel and Eck, 1994), community policing models have grown very popular in recent decades and have "become the new orthodoxy for cops" (Eck and Rosenbaum, 2000, p. 30).

What constitutes "community policing"? Though there is no clear definition, most practitioners and researchers would agree with Trojano-wicz et al. (1998, p. 3) that community policing is "based on the concept that police officers and private citizens working together in creative ways can help solve contemporary community problems related to crime, fear of crime, social and physical disorder, and neighborhood conditions."

The basic philosophy of COP is that increasing the quality and quantity of contacts between citizens and police to resolve community concerns can enhance community life. This requires the police to react quickly to urgent demands, engage and empower communities to deal with their own problems, and collaborate with the community to address community concerns (Trojanowicz and Bucqueroux, 1998). The central premise of COP is that "the public should be seen along with the police as 'coproducers of safety and order'" (Skolnick and Bayley, 1988, p. 5).

Skogan and Hartnett (1997) contend the central philosophy and premise of COP lead to four general principles

- organizational decentralization and a reorientation of patrol to facilitate communication and information sharing between the police and the public
- a broad commitment to problem-oriented policing — that is, "a comprehensive plan for improving policing in which a high priority attached to addressing substantive problems shapes the police agency, influencing all changes in personnel, organization, and procedures" (Goldstein, 1990, p. 32) — that analyzes problems systematically to develop more effective means of addressing them (Goldstein, 1987)
- police consideration of community issues and priorities in tactic development
- police commitment to assisting communities to solve problems on their own

The six most common principles of COP Kelling and Coles (1996) identify are

- belief in a broad policing function beyond law enforcement
- acknowledgment that the police rely on citizens in many ways

- recognition that police work is complex and requires general knowledge, skill, and discretion
- reliance on specific tactics targeted at problems and developed with the community rather than general tactics such as preventive patrol and rapid response
- devolution of police authority to lower levels to respond to neighborhood needs
- commitment of police to serve multiple aims from reducing crime and fear to helping citizens manage problems

Skolnick and Bayley (1988) similarly find community-based crime prevention, reorientation of patrol activities to emphasize nonemergency services, increased accountability to the public, and decentralization of command to be recurring themes of community policing. Such principles describe a police role that is broad in objective and function and that derives authority from and requires collaboration with the community.

Measuring Community Policing

The rather broad and varying definitions that have been offered for community policing have led to myriad methods for measuring it. The simplest measurement of COP is the claim of an agency to have implemented it (e.g., Maguire, 1997).

A more common technique identifies criteria associated with COP and combines them to form indexes or scales. Using COPS FAST (Funding Accelerated for Small Towns) data from the COPS Office, Maguire et al. (1997) constructed an index of thirty-one activities (e.g., COP training for citizens and officers, writing a COP plan, community-oriented foot or bicycle patrols) to gauge COP among agencies in their sample. Zhao (1996, p. 44) used indexes to measure COP "external" activities for "the reorientation of police operations and crime prevention activities" (e.g., more officers on foot or bicycle, special task units for problem-solving, crime education) and "internal" activities involving "innovations in police management" (e.g., increased hiring of civilians for non-law enforcement tasks, reassessment of ranks and regulations). Zhao, Thurman, and Lovrich (1995) also used the "external" index to measure the facilitators and impediments of COP.

More recent measurements of COP have used factor analytic techniques.[1] In a study of innovation in 432 of the largest U.S. police organizations, King (1998) assessed two associated with COP. "Radical innovation" measurements indicated whether an organization had both implemented COP and had officers assigned to it. "Community policing programmatic innovation" measurements included community crime prevention and foot patrols. While community crime prevention was found to be positively associated with the innovation measurements, foot patrols were found to have a negative relationship with them. Theoretically, both measures should have had a positive influence; King's results may indicate foot patrol is a poor measure of COP or that there were other confounding issues in his model. King's model could not take advantage of other measures such as crime analysis and Drug Abuse Resistance Education (DARE), which are both community-oriented activities that could have been used to enhance the measurement of COP implementation. In subsequent research, King (2000) included school drug education as a component of COP programmatic innovation.

Like King, Maguire and Mastrofski (2000) find exploratory factor analysis useful for measuring COP, particularly given the numerous schemes for identifying the dimensions of COP and the difficulty of constructing a confirmatory analysis model with a large number of variables. Their analysis extracts factors from three COPS samples and one from the Police Foundation, carefully basing calculations on the appropriate tetrachoric and polychoric correlations.[2] They found a single dimension of COP in the three COPS datasets but five such dimensions in the Police Foundation data, including those pertaining to explicit COP activities (e.g., surveying and training citizens), patrol officer activities (e.g., making door-to-door contacts), citizen activities (e.g., citizens helping develop police policy), midlevel manager issues (e.g., whether midlevel managers make decisions about prioritizing problems), and organizational structure (e.g., decentralization of field services and investigations).[3] These findings suggest the number of COP dimensions could range from one to five, but it is unclear whether these dimensions are measures of a single latent construct of COP. In addition, as Maguire and Mastrofski concede, exploratory factor analysis is atheoretical.

The atheoretical nature of exploratory factor analysis diminishes its utility for measuring COP. Exploratory factor analysis capitalizes on data idiosyncrasies, which may help explain why studies of different data using it have not produced consistent results. This leaves researchers the task of explaining why certain measures might not affect COP as other similar or related ones do. Furthermore, if exploratory factor analysis is used simply to identify measures that can be pooled together, it does not take advantage of related measures that could enhance the measurement of a particular construct. As noted earlier, DARE was highly related to King's (1998) COP programmatic dimension, but the technique precluded him from using it as a measure of that dimension because it also affected another dimension of policing. In comparing results of these studies, it would be informative to measure COP using confirmatory factor analytic techniques because they permit the testing of theoretically derived dimensions and measures.

Nevertheless, past research using exploratory factor analysis and other means has provided valuable insight for ways to improve the measurement of COP implementation. One improvement would be a measure of COP implementation that

- is measured on an interval level scale
- accounts for varying levels of implementation
- accounts for measurement error of indicators
- accounts for nominal, ordinal, and interval data in construction of a composite measure
- accounts for multiple types of COP-related activities
- allows the empirical comparison of police organizations implementing COP in various forms
- empirically gauges the extent to which COP implementation varies for police organizations across time or place, and
- has been statistically validated on multiple samples of data

This research seeks to determine whether a measure of community policing implementation can be derived that overcomes limitations of previous studies. Capitalizing on the findings of previous studies, especially in terms of measurement, permits the construction of confirmatory measurement models that may provide better estimates of COP implementation that are also theoretically informed and testable. I seek to develop and test such a model in this book. The model is subject to several data limitations, but it demonstrates an approach that future research may consider.

The Importance of Measuring Implementation

Few studies have focused specifically on establishing a measure of COP implementation. Most COP research comprises case studies (Greene, 1993), with empirical studies treating COP as something to be explained (i.e., a dependent variable) or something that determines some other concept of interest (i.e., an independent variable). This is particularly evident in studies of community policing that discuss whether police organization structure influences COP implementation (e.g., King, 2000; Zhao, 1996) or if implementation of community policing alters the structure of the police organization (e.g., Maguire, 1997). COP research has generally focused either on COP values and change in general or the impact of COP programs (Zhao et al., 1995). The results of these studies often conflict or are not replicated, possibly due to measurement issues.[4]

As noted, since 1994 the COPS Office has provided about $11.3 billion for local COP implementation (COPS, 2005). Even the few works that have assessed the impact of this funding, however, have not done so directly. For example, Zhao, Scheider, and Thurman (2002) found COPS funding was associated with crime reduction in medium- and large-size cities. The implicit assumption of their work was that agencies used grants to perform actual COP activities. Without directly measuring COP implementation, it is not possible to conclude whether it was COP or the ability to use COP funds for other activities (e.g., hiring officers to conduct COP but who actually undertook traditional law enforcement activities) that led to the reductions in crime that Zhao et al. found. Muhlhausen's (2001) finding that COPS hiring and redeployment grants had no discernible effect on violence demonstrate the importance of measuring how COP is implemented, as do the findings of Davis, Muhlhausen, Ingram, and Rector (2000) that

COPS grants frequently did not produce the required officers to fill the funded positions. In other words, COPS funding has been used for something, but not necessarily as intended. Funding alone is not a good measure of COP implementation. A more direct measure of COP implementation is needed to demonstrate whether COP funding can achieve its goals if properly used.

This work seeks to develop a useful, more direct measure or framework for measuring COP implementation. Such a measure should help ascertain the extent of COP implementation for policing as a whole, as well as for individual agencies. It can help practitioners gauge their progress in implementing COP and help scholars compare multiple organizations across time. Such a tool would also permit a better assessment of the facilitators and impediments of COP implementation as well as its impact on public safety. Though this effort may not result in an absolute, definitive measure of COP implementation, it should serve as a step toward developing future measures with still greater utility.

Research on Implementation

At its most basic level, this book is a study of implementation. As a field of scholarly inquiry, implementation has developed only recently and sporadically. Pressman and Wildavsky found the field to be virtually nonexistent in 1973. Williams (1976) noted the lack of concern for implementation impeded the improvement of social policy. Though some (Kelman, 1984) claim implementation has advanced since Pressman and Wildavsky's seminal research, others contend it has lost clarity and meaning (Linder and Peters, 1987), that its consequence is small and lacks a coherent theory (Alexander, 1985; Berman, 1980, deLeon, 1999b), and that it has become "stuck in a rut" (Salamon, 1981, p. 256).

Several obstacles have hindered the progress of implementation research. Lester, Bowman, Goggin, and O'Toole (1987) contend it has been impeded by the inadequacies of theoretical pluralism (i.e., too many theories with little consensus), restrictive studies (e.g., in terms of time, number, policy type, definition of implementation, and approach), and a limited accumulation of research. Others agree the theoretical formulation of implementation research needs further work. Maitland (1995), in referring to O'Toole's (1986) review of more

than 100 implementation studies that uncovered over 300 key variables, claims implementation research needs a theoretical structure
(which he attempted to provide by developing a taxonomy of implementation types based upon ambiguity and conflict).[5]

Most researchers agree implementation research has value, but that
its development over time has been tumultuous. More specifically,
there is a consensus about four aspects of implementation research.
First, there is considerable research in many journals either about or
related to implementation that is not labeled as such (Meier, 1999;
Winter, 1999; O'Toole, 2000). These studies could be used to guide
current implementation research. Second, there appears to be agreement on developing more specific concepts pertaining to broad classes
of policies that would be more precise than universal schemes (Schneider, 1999; Winter). Third, there is agreement that implementation
efforts should not be judged as a "success" or "failure," but rather on a
continuum (Lester and Goggin, 1998; Schneider; Winter).

Fourth and finally, there is agreement that there should be greater
emphasis on statistical and comparative approaches to implementation
rather than case studies in implementation research (deLeon, 1999a;
Meier, 1999; Winter, 1999; O'Toole, 2000). Although they have value,
particularly in the detail they offer, reliance on case studies raises a number of concerns. Conducting such studies is resource intensive, which
frequently makes them difficult to conduct in practice. Yin (1982), for
example, found "exemplary" implementation studies included unstruc-
tured discussion, structured interviews, participant observation, and
field observation, activities that generally limit the sample that can be
examined. It is also difficult to determine "equivalence" between programs in small sample studies, particularly where there is no common
structure among the studies and given evidence that may make differences between programs that may be less critical than they appear. The
inability to determine equivalency also inhibits theory construction.
Dryzek and Ripley (1988) contend ambitious designs require greater
demands on social science theory. The limited theoretical development
of implementation research therefore limits the ability to develop and
use better research designs for it. Improving the ability to determine
"equivalence" and hypothesis testing would also contribute to greater

generalizability in implementation research. Goggin's (1986) criticism that implementation studies tend to favor the examination of a few cases is an indication that generalizability is lacking in implementation research. The failure to determine equivalency also hinders the accumulation of knowledge — a criticism that Palumbo (1987) claims is characteristic to the field.

Small sample studies also make it difficult to ascertain the causes of program success or failure. As Goggin (1986) explains, using one or a small number of cases make it difficult to control for spurious or confounding variables that threaten internal validity of the studies. By failing to control for such variables, case studies make it difficult to determine whether outcomes are a result of the program or policy implemented or some other variable. Small samples make it difficult to isolate which determinants are crucial for implementation success or even facilitation. Empirical analyses can focus more precisely on such determinants (Meier, 1999).

Overcoming Prior Limitations

This book undertakes several steps to advance implementation research in ways researchers discussed above have advocated. First, I draw on literature regarding organizational theory, innovation, and policing. Not all this literature may be explicitly associated with implementation, but all can inform the study of COP implementation. Second, from this literature I derive and classify into categories determinants that transcend COP implementation and could be studied in relation to a class of policies (e.g., implementation of policies and activities by criminal justice agencies). Third, I use multiple measures to form measurement models that can be statistically validated, provide weighted estimates from multiple variables, and account for measurement error. Through these advanced analytical techniques, I am able to obtain more precise representations of implementation and its antecedents. Fourth, using these modeling techniques, I construct an interval-level continuum of COP implementation that is superior to dichotomous representations and provides a mechanism to account for partial implementation. Finally, I examine large, longitudinal samples of policing organizations, allowing comparisons over time and place. This helps increase theory development and the accumulation of knowledge by treating the organizations as equivalent for the purposes of comparison, increasing the validity of model and hypothesis testing, improving the ability to account for several independent influences so that important ones can be isolated and precisely estimated, and enhancing generalizability.

3

POLICE ORGANIZATIONS AS OPEN SYSTEMS

Although traditional notions of police organization are grounded in a closed-model perspective, emphasizing the autonomy of the police from the community, there is growing recognition that police organizations are increasingly open systems. This perspective has featured in the work of numerous scholars (e.g., Langworthy, 1986; Maguire, 1997 and 2003; Maguire et al., 1997; Mastrofski, 1998; Zhao, 1996). I follow these researchers in considering police organizations and COP in light of an open systems framework because of its comprehensiveness, utility, and intuitive appeal.

An open systems framework outlines the basic elements of the organizational context (features of the organization and its environment that affect its form and function), and provides a foundation for considering the relationship between organizational context, structure, and implementation of COP. Because this framework is fundamental to this research, I provide some historical background on it before I describe contingency and institutional theory, the two primary theories based on the open systems framework that are used in this research. Finally, I offer a critical assessment of these theories.

Historical Development of the Open Systems Framework

Open systems may be first considered a framework for system-based theories. A system is a set of interlocking elements that acquires inputs from the environment, transforms them, and discharges the outputs to the external environment in the form of goods and services (Daft, 2001). Thompson (1967) was the first to distinguish between closed and open systems, arguing that closed systems are relatively autonomous from the external environment, whereas open systems must constantly interact with their environments.

Daft (2001) argues organizations in general are shifting from mechanical, closed systems to more biological, open systems. The increasingly complex and unpredictable context in which organizations must operate was recognized in the Hawthorne studies of the 1920s and 1930s and their demonstration of the importance of social needs and informal organizations in the workplace, as well as in Maslow's (1943) theory of motivation. The discovery that factors outside the control of organizations play a role in organizational function and form led theorists such as Katz and Kahn (1966) and Lawrence and Lorsch (1967) to consider organizations as open systems, and Morgan (1997) to liken open system organizations to organisms depending on both context and internal subsystems. As an open system, the organizational structure and activities within a police agency depend on these contextual and internal features within the organizational context.

There are two theories based on the open systems framework that are particularly enlightening on how organizational context may affect police organization activities. These are contingency theory and institutional theory. Contingency theory describes the task environment of organizations. Institutional theory describes the environment of expectations of organizations. Together, the task and institutional environments form the context of police organizations.

Contingency Theory

A contingency is a characteristic or event that depends on another. A contingency model of COP implementation can be considered as a theoretical framework that considers COP implementation as a function of an organization's task environment, structural dimensions, and the congruence among them. Donaldson (1987) classifies this generally as an adaptive cycle. An organization is in fit when its structure is well-designed for the task environment in which it operates. When changes in its contingency variables produce misfit, or an incongruence between the organizational structure and the task environment, organizational performance decreases. The structure must then be altered to reduce the misfit and restore equilibrium and performance. As do all contingency theories, this assumes organizations rationally pursue effective performance.

Although contingency theory views organizations as open, organic systems, it also contends the most appropriate form of organization depends on the task environment. As such, organizations can be considered on a continuum between mechanical and organic. Burns and Stalker (1961) found that organizations operating in a stable environment tend to have mechanical structures, while those operating in uncertain and turbulent environments adopted organic structures. Lawrence and Lorsch (1967) likewise found organizational variables form a complex interrelationship with one another and with the conditions in the task environment.

Identifying that police work is to a large extent nonroutine and occurs in an unstable, complex environment, Cordner (1978) was among the first to contend open models are more appropriate for police organizations. This followed Angell's (1971, 1975, and 1976) proposals for democratic models of police organization to help overcome many problems, such as poor community relations, low employee morale, and coordination and control of tasks inherent in traditional police organizations. As open systems, the structure, policies, practices, and activities of police organizations would depend on contingencies that exist within the task environment. I will later discuss these in more depth.

Institutional Theory

The basic tenet of institutional theories is that organizations are social systems shaped by the social, cultural, and symbolic systems in which they are situated, rather than tools structured for effective work (Donaldson, 1995). In other words, organizations are shaped by elements such as ideas, expectations, opinions, accepted knowledge, and laws in the surrounding environment regarding the proper structure and activities for the organization, rather than by concerns for coordination and control that lead to technical efficiency and effectiveness. These influences comprise the institutional environment of the organizational context. Meyer and Rowan (1977) refer to such ideas and beliefs as "myths" to which organizations must ceremonially conform to appear appropriate and responsible.[1] Ceremonial activity has ritualistic importance because it maintains appearances and provides validation for the organization (Meyer and Rowan). Consequently, organizational success and survival ultimately rest on the ability of the organization to conform to the demands of the institutional environment. Myths about acceptable ways of thinking that have become legitimized (e.g., sanctioned by a professional association or the state) have the greatest impact on organizational operations. In a constant pursuit of legitimacy, organizations respond to these pressures by conducting activities that coincide with institutional expectations.[2]

Crank (1994) credits Sorel (1916) with the idea that myths are ideas held by particular groups attempting social change. Myths are both "social" and "political" in that participants collectively hold them and seek to influence change. They are "intentional" rather than reflective because they act on social structure, and "magical" because they are not assessable within the realm of rational choice (Strenski, 1987).

Crank (1994) summarizes four common elements to myths: (1) they are powerful, (2) the affected environment contextualizes them, (3) they have an inherent notion of emergence or change, and (4) they are championed by powerful individuals or political interest groups. Crank contends COP is based on the myths of "watchman" and "community." Such myths are powerful because both the community and police agree these are appropriate models for police organizations and activities. The myths are contextualized as neighborhoods are defined geographically and ethnically. They evoke change as the image of urban environments transforms from one of decay and danger to a safe and secure "community" protected by a "watchman." Finally, these myths have been championed by pioneering researchers such as Wilson (1968) and Wilson and Kelling (1982), who acted as institutional entrepreneurs.

Criticisms of the Open Systems Framework

Although an open systems framework is useful for comparing police organizations, it does have some shortcomings. Among these are the extent of contingencies and unfalsifiable theory and the lack of integration within and among theories. I discuss these and other shortcomings below.

Extent of Contingencies and Unfalsifiable Theory

An undesirable property of an open systems framework is that the number and type of contingencies that may influence an organization are endless. In other words, these theories essentially argue "it all depends," which elicits the logical response and criticism "on what?". Among the most studied organizational characteristics based on the open systems framework are organization size and age, technology, environment, and institutional elements, a list that is far from exhaustive. Among environmental properties, for example, Rainey (1991) adds law, economics, and ecology. Strategy, goals, management, and leadership of the organization are also important elements. The list of potentially relevant elements is without bound.

The point is that the number of important properties cannot be established, which makes disproving the open systems framework a futile exercise. Any test of it that failed to find a relationship between a contextual and an organizational element could simply conclude the wrong elements were included in the model. Any variable not typically considered by a theory based on the framework that was found to be associated with an organizational property could be reinterpreted as another important element and support for a general open systems framework.

Despite these deficiencies, the open systems framework is useful for the present research because it is possible to determine whether specific contextual properties are important predictors of structure and COP implementation. Neither the framework nor the theories based on it are being tested here because organizational outcomes (e.g., effectiveness measures) are not the focus of this work. Rather, the theories contribute to a testable open systems model that may be useful for explaining the implementation of COP in police organizations. This work follows the approach of several other scholars who have employed this general approach in the study of police organizations (e.g., Langworthy, 1986; Maguire, 2003; Zhao, 1996).

Lack of Integration Among and Within Theories

Theories based on the open systems framework are also limited by their lack of integration with each other. This is particularly true of "contingency" and "institutional" theories founded on seemingly conflicting assumptions. Donaldson (1995) in particular notes that organizational theory has failed to build upon contingency theory and to integrate it with other contemporary theories such as population ecology theory, institutional theory, resource dependency theory, and organizational economics.[3] Pfeffer (1993) echoes this criticism that the field of organizational theory has a low level of paradigm development, and he acknowledges the more important point that lack of consensus inhibits the advancement of knowledge. Recall these are the same criticisms made about implementation and community policing research.

Theories of organizations need not be mutually exclusive. Though contingency and institutional fields are often thought to be so, in fact one might interpret institutional demands as another contingency organizations must consider, and satisfying institutional expectations as another measure of effectiveness. In other words, these theories may complement each other as Donaldson (1995) contends. Although not typically categorized with them, institutional theories are just as much a part of the open systems framework as contingency theories. A commonly held proposition of both contingency and institutional theories is that organizations operate within a context that ultimately affects how organizations structure themselves and go about their activities. The difference between these theories lies primarily in whether organizations are assumed to respond to contextual demands for rationality or legitimacy. Contingency theory suggests organizations are concerned with aligning structures and activities with the demands of the organizational context to maximize their performance. Institutional theory suggests organizations design their structure and activities to maximize consistency with myths and expectations arising from the institutional environment of the organizational context.

Zucker (1987) observes that institutional ideas are usually tested against "rational" perspectives. Although some may consider institutional theories to be theories of "irrational" behavior, responses to institutional expectations are a rational endeavor, and there are institutional pressures to be effective. Organizations that do not adhere to such influences and expectations may find it more difficult, if not impossible, to accomplish performance objectives. Those able to satisfy institutional stakeholders and gain legitimacy may discover that doing so enhances their effectiveness. If success is defined to include survival, then the pursuit of performance and legitimacy are both rational endeavors necessary for survival. That is, organizational structure and activities may both be rational responses to requirements for production and conformity to institutional pressures. This suggests factors pertaining to both the task and institutional environments comprise an organization's context and ultimately influence how the organization is structured and what activities it implements. Contingency theories on how organizations maximize their performance and institutional theories on how organizations deal with traditional expectations are not at odds when one considers institutional demands to be another contingency organizations must address.

Acknowledging that organizations must address both rational-technical and legitimating concerns is not a new notion. Organizational scholars have acknowledged the utility of organizational structure models encompassing both. Parsons (1961), for example, considers three components of organizational structure. The first is the adaptation organizations make to obtain the resources necessary to conduct their activities and accomplish their goals. This includes the way resources are pooled and organized to accomplish organization objectives. The second is institutionalized pressures transforming resources into processes that lead to goal attainment. This includes both marketing the organizational product and implementing organizational goals, both of which are governed by the "operative code" founded in the value system of the organization. The third component is decision-making and setting organization commitments.

Donaldson (1995) claims Parsons's (1961) first component corresponds to a technical level for conducting work, the second to an institutional level for legitimating the organization based on shared societal values, and the third to a managerial level that coordinates the work and the technical and institutional levels. He argues institutional theory only emphasizes the institutional component of the Parsonian model of organizations to the detriment of other components. In his view (p. 119), "The institutional function is not just a function, but becomes *the* function whose logic governs all else [emphasis in original]."

Donaldson's (1995) criticism of institutional theory may also be applied to contingency theory. Contingency theory emphasizes the role of the task environment without acknowledging any function the institutional environment might have in determining organizational function and form. Either theory is misspecified without the other.

Other theorists, including institutional theorists, have also acknowledged the presence of both technical and institutional demands (e.g., Hirsch, 1975; Meyer and Rowan, 1977; Meyer and Scott, 1983). Meyer and Rowan contend that formal structures of organizations develop from two contexts. One context includes the encouragement of structures that facilitate coordination and control of production by local relational networks. The other context is highly institutional and arises from the interconnectedness of societal relations, the collective organization of society, and organizational leadership. Although the technical demands for efficiency often conflict with the demands from institutional environments, every organization is embedded within both contexts. As a result, organizations must be concerned with both the technical aspects of coordinating and controlling their activities as well as the institutional aspects of accounting for them. Some organizations, Meyer and Rowan contend, depend more on technical demands while others depend more on institutional demands; organizations can be placed on a continuum where success is determined by the extent to which they must adhere to production relative to institutional requirements.

Some theorists have sought to reconcile technical-rational and institutional models of organization in policing research. Mastrofski (1998) recognized that police organizations operate at both technical and institutional levels, and that support for COP came from both contexts. COP is considered by those interested in police effectiveness to be an improvement over the reform or professional model of policing (Kelling and Coles, 1996; Kelling and Moore, 1988). At the same time, Crank (1994) claims, COP (like most models of policing) adheres to institutionalized myths that the police should act as watchmen protecting communities. Because police organizations are embedded within both technical and institutional environments (and both environments support COP), it is not surprising that the choices police organizations make to implement COP (or any other organizational activity) reflect influences from both environments.

Mastrofski (1998) also characterizes the consequences of four structural changes championed by COP reforms resulting from the influences of technical and institutional contexts. These are delayerization, professionalization of police officers, democratizing of the police, and police integration with local government services.

Delayerization reduces the number of middle managers, which, Mastrofski (1998) claims, may not have much impact on effectiveness because middle managers typically have little influence over line activities. Delayerization, if it has been deemed proper, may help legitimize the organization, but would reduce opportunities for advancement, and thereby reduce the commitment of officers to the organization.

Professionalization of police officers (e.g., giving police officers the power to make decisions regarding the best methods of obtaining organizational objectives as well as the skill and support to do so) will only influence the technical capacity of the organization to the extent the decisions that officers make are effective. Nevertheless, this change is widely accepted because many support personal and decisive actions by officers.

Democratizing the police occurs by making them partners with the community (e.g., identifying and solving community problems together). Organizational effectiveness will increase only to the extent that democratization or partnership is implemented, and, if implemented, only if the police and the public work to increase effectiveness. Regardless of how it increases effectiveness, the notion of democratization or a partnership can increase the legitimacy of police organizations because of the institutional support for citizen accountability and government responsiveness.

Police helping to integrate local government services places the organization in a high-risk situation, but such attempts can enhance effectiveness. This can also satisfy institutional demands for an integrated, holistic form of local government that pursues citizen interests.

Mastrofski's (1998) observations illustrate how police operate in both technical and institutional environments. Because police organizations make decisions in both environments, they must be aware of the demands of both environments. It is therefore appropriate for a model of COP implementation (or any other police initiative) to account for both technical and institutional demands placed on the organization. Such a model would simultaneously draw on both contingency and institutional theories.

Models of policing work should consider the relationship of multiple, rather than single, contextual dimensions with organizational elements. Early organizational studies tended to be narrow in scope, focusing on single dimensions such as organization size, technology, or environment. This was likely due to the infancy of organizational theories at the time. Relatively recent organizational studies, particularly those pertaining to police organizations, illustrate the integration of multiple dimensions (e.g., Langworthy, 1986; Zhao, 1994; Maguire, 2003). None of these studies can be considered exhaustive, because no study can identify every single contingency that might have predictive power.

4

ORGANIZATIONAL CONTEXT AND COMMUNITY POLICING

Just as previous research has provided insight on measuring COP implementation, it has also offered clues on the variables that influence it. Some of these elements constitute the organizational context for police agencies. This book seeks to identify elements of this organizational context that not only determine the structure of police agencies, but also facilitate or inhibit the implementation of COP. Contingency theories (based on task environment) and institutional theories (based on institutional environment) comprise the theoretical underpinning for most such studies. Having reviewed the basic components of these theories and their application to police work in previous chapters,

I turn to how task and institutional elements of organizational context may affect COP implementation.

Task Environment

Contingency theorists have identified several characteristics of the task environment that affect organizations and may be important determinants of COP implementation. These include organization size and age, technology, and environmental (or community) characteristics. I review the literature on the association of each of these characteristics with COP implementation.

Organization Size

Blau (1970) and Blau and Schoenherr (1971) were among the first to acknowledge the importance of size in shaping organizational structure. Blau's theory of organizational differentiation is that organization size enhances differentiation, but the impact is less as size increases. Further, greater differentiation leads to a larger administrative component for coordination.[1] The relationship between size and structure has been well supported in subsequent studies (e.g., Child, 1973a; Hsu, Marsh, and Mannari, 1983; Meyer, 1972); Meyer claimed, "one cannot underestimate the impact of size on other characteristics of organizations" (p. 440).

It is reasonable to expect the size of an organization to affect not only its structure, but also its functions and activities — including, for police organizations, COP implementation. Maguire et al. (1997) suggest the influence of department size on the adoption of COP may be bi-directional. That is, larger departments may be better suited to implement COP because of their greater pool of resources, while smaller communities may prefer a broader array of functions from the police (see also Flanagan, 1985). The limited evidence available suggests the effect of greater resources outweighs community preferences. Maguire et al. found, in a sample of 5,726 nonurban, local police agencies applying for COPS funding, that larger police agencies have implemented COP to a greater extent than smaller ones. Zhao (1996) also found city size to be positively related to external (e.g., use of storefront police stations, block watch programs) and internal (e.g., hiring civilians, group problem-solving) changes focused toward COP. King (1998), however, found no association in a sample of the 432 largest U.S. police agencies between organization or city size and either COP programmatic innovation or radical COP implementation (including both COP implementation and regular assignment of community officers).

Organization Age

Scholars have debated the effect of age on organizational effectiveness. Ranger-Moore (1997) summarizes competing perspectives that contend either (1) a liability of newness (Stinchcombe, 1965), (2) a liability of adolescence (Levinthal and Fichman, 1988; Brüderl and Schüssler, 1990), or (3) a liability of aging (Meyer 1990; Meyer and Brown, 1977). The explanations of these effects range from experience and learning curves, to resources and to enthusiasm, and ossification. Contrary to police organizations that are generally much older and do not "fail" in the market sense, these studies are based on private firms of wide-varying ages that can effectively fail. The applicability of these findings to the police is not entirely clear. It seems plausible, however, that older police organizations have more experience to draw on, which may provide them a greater capacity to make informed decisions. They would therefore choose to organize according to what their experience suggests to them may or may not work. To the extent that age has provided experience supporting its likely effectiveness, older police organizations may be more supportive of COP. Their experience may have also provided lessons on conducting COP-like activities, which may facilitate implementation. Only King (1998) has explored the age–COP relationship. He found organization age to be positively related to COP programmatic innovation, but to have no impact on radical COP innovation.

Task Scope

Technology is a contextual dimension representing the set of tools and techniques used to transform organization inputs into outputs (Perrow, 1967). The output of police organizations is service to the community. The technology of police organizations produces an intangible output that is labor and knowledge intensive, customer-oriented, and immediately consumed (i.e., service is used immediately and cannot be stored or accumulated). Given emphasis on the customer, service technology requires technical core employees to be close to the customer. This often makes the organization more decentralized and less formal. Moreover, the employee skill level must be high, particularly for interpersonal relations.

Perrow (1967) argued that technology is a function of task variety and analyzability. Task variety refers to the frequency of exceptions or unique events that occur and must be handled. Task analyzability depends on whether the conversion of inputs to outputs is logical and analytic, or based on experience and intuition. An organization uses nonroutine technology when it experiences many unique events and tasks are based on experience and intuition. It uses routine technology when it faces few exceptions and is able to employ a logical and analytic approach to its processes.

If COP is a nonroutine technology, as Maguire (2003) suggests, and can be measured by community-based activities conducted by the organization, it may be a function of task scope. More specifically, the implementation of COP may be facilitated by increased task scope resulting from the need to provide additional service to citizens in a manner that is easier for them to access. This is consistent with the general proposition of the open systems framework that considers organizations to be in constant interaction with their context.

Community Characteristics

Organizational studies frequently discuss the role of the "environment" in shaping organizations. In the context of police work, the community represents the environment for the organization, with uncertainty in the community equivalent to uncertainty in the "environment." Uncertainty in a community is a function of complexity, and stability, the degree to which environmental factors change over time (Duncan, 1972).[2]

Burns and Stalker (1961) found that organizations that operated in stable environments were very formal and mechanistic, while those that operated in unstable environments had internal structures that were informal, organic, and adaptive. This suggests police organizations in complex, unstable environments may be more likely to implement COP in response to community needs. Thompson (1967), however, contends organizations will seal off their core technologies when the external environment is uncertain. This suggests organizations in more complex and unstable environments will have more complex structures and elaborate control mechanisms to buffer the organization from uncertainty. Such conditions may place competing demands on the police, making it more difficult for them to garner support and introduce new programs such as COP.

Because the number and type of issues occurring within a community are closely associated with its disorganization, constructs associated with social disorganization can help to gauge community uncertainty. Shaw and McKay (1972) identify community heterogeneity, socioeconomic status, and population mobility as key components of community disorganization. Heterogeneity and mobility make it difficult for communities to integrate socially, thereby causing uncertainty in the problems that may arise from diversity. Such uncertainty, when tied to decreasing socioeconomic status of community residents, is also tied to decreasing resources for police to address problems. Social disorganization theory provides constructs that are consistent with more general components of uncertainty as well as those associated with crime, delinquency, and other problems prompting police action.

The role of community characteristics in explaining COP is unclear. Zhao's (1996) study of COP change found support for the relationship between social disorganization and the adoption of COP. All eight of his measures of social disorganization were statistically related to external change toward COP, and three of the eight were associated with internal change toward COP.[3] King (1998), however, found similar measures to be unrelated to COP. He found the proportion of households headed by nonmarried persons influenced radical COP innovation but not programmatic COP innovation, and none of the other measures to be related to either of his COP measures.

The studies of environment and police organizations are far from definitive. Many studies suggest community characteristics affect COP implementation and police organizational structure, but the evidence even for this is not overwhelming (I discuss some of these in Chapter 6). Further work is needed before anything definitive can be said about community uncertainty and the structure and activities of police organizations.

Institutional Environment

Like contingency theorists, institutional theorists have identified several elements of the institutional environment that influence organizations and may explain variation in COP implementation. Sources of institutional expectations may include the environmental capacity of the organization, funding incentives, and region. Below, I review studies addressing the relationships between these variables and COP implementation.

Environmental Capacity

Maguire (2003) refers to "environmental capacity" as the ability of police organizations to act independently of third-party organizations. He composed an index of environmental capacity based on the influence of civil service boards, employee unions, citizen review panels, and accreditation status. Although he found this measure had no relationship with organizational structure (as I will discuss in Chapter 6), King's (1998) work suggests it could possibly influence COP implementation.

King (1998) examined how civil service and unionization may explain COP innovation. He found where the police were civil service employees, they were less likely to adopt radical COP innovation, but this characteristic was unrelated to COP programmatic innovation. Whether the police had a union was unassociated with either of his measures of COP innovation. Additional empirical research on "environmental capacity" and COP innovation would be useful.

Funding Incentives

Funding incentives are another potential source of influence on COP implementation. They may exert institutional pressures on police organizations to act and organize in specific ways. For example, funding incentives may be a pecuniary enticement to adopt practices deemed proper by some institutional agent. To date, this relationship does not appear to have been explored empirically. This variable, however, is also indicative of resource dependency theory. This theory, also based on the open systems framework, assumes that organizations respond to demands and expectations placed on them by sources on which they depend for sustenance (Pfeffer and Salancik, 1978). Importantly, both theories recognize the importance of this variable as a potential predictor of COP implementation, and that it should be included in the model — but since it is indicative of both theories, any finding regarding it cannot be considered evidence for the efficacy of any one theory. This is fine for the context of this book because my intent is not to test theory, but rather is to use theory to construct a model that is helpful for explaining COP implementation.

Region

Geographic region may influence COP implementation to the extent that residents of different regions have different expectations of police activities, thereby exerting different institutional pressures. Maguire et al. (1997) criticize past research for not providing a reasonable explanation of region. From a review of policing literature, they conclude the importance of region for police work stems from regional differences in political structures (Wilson, 1968), historical development of the police (Langworthy and Travis, 1994), and innovation diffusion networks (Weiss 1992 and 1997). For example, Weiss has shown empirically that risk mediation (i.e., the organization's desire to reduce its risk of civil liability), cosmopolitanism (i.e., participation of police executives in policy communities), and peer emulation (i.e., the extent to which innovation is influenced by communication and imitation) are important for understanding innovativeness (i.e., the number of innovations adopted and the organization's reputation for innovativeness). To the extent that these characteristics vary by region and community policing is a form of innovativeness, regional effects may be a function of these qualities.

Though region is sometimes overlooked in analyses of variation in police organizational structures, some studies have examined its relationship to COP. Maguire et al. (1997) found police agencies in the Western region of the United States were most likely to implement COP, followed by those in the Northeast, South, and Midwest. Zhao (1996) found no differences by region in terms of external change toward COP, but that agencies in the Central and Northeast regions implemented fewer internal COP functions than those in the Midwest and South.

5

ORGANIZATIONAL STRUCTURE AND COMMUNITY POLICING

Much contemporary discussion of organizational structure stems from the ideas of Weber (1946) on bureaucracy and of Blau (1970) and Blau and Schoenherr (1971) on differentiation. Weber characterized modern bureaucracy as having a division of responsibility, hierarchy of authority, and educated officials who manage according to written documents. Blau considered formal structure to represent differentiation within the organization. He writes

> A dimension of differentiation is any criterion on the basis of which the members of an organization are divided into positions, as illustrated by the division of labor, or into ranks, notably managerial

levels, or into subunits, such as local branches, headquarters, divisions, or sections within branches or divisions. (p. 203)

In other words, Blau saw organizational structure as how an organization defined itself functionally, occupationally, hierarchically, and spatially.

Scholars had begun, prior to Blau, to define various dimensions of organizational structure. Pugh et al. (1961) outlined six dimensions of organizational structure evident in the literature: specialization, standardization, formalization, centralization, configuration, and flexibility. Specialization refers to the division of labor within an organization; Pugh et al. noted both the number of functions performed by specialists as well as differentiation within each function as indicators of specialization. Standardization refers to procedures for handling events occurring with regularity as well as various roles within the organization. Formalization refers to the extent of written policies for communication and procedure. Centralization refers to the hierarchical level that has the authority to make decisions; centralized organizations are those where decision-making occurs at upper levels of the organizational hierarchy.[1] Configuration is the dimension of the structure, essentially the relationship between positions regarding lines of authority and responsibility of subordinates (e.g., vertical and horizontal spans of control). Flexibility describes changes an organization makes over a given amount of time.[2]

Recent research of organizational structure has retained the basic tenets of earlier research. Daft (2001) contends organizational structure can be viewed through six cardinal aspects. Four of these — including specialization, hierarchy of authority, centralization, and formalization — reflect those of Pugh et al. (1963) and Blau (1970). A fifth, professionalism, reflects Weber's (1946) similar notion that officials within formal bureaucracies be trained, educated, and qualified for their positions. A sixth, personnel ratios (the number of employees assigned to specific tasks as a proportion of all employees in an organization), is essentially what Blau called the administrative component of organizations.[3]

Several studies of police organizational structure have used these concepts. The most well known is Langworthy's (1986) empirical analysis of police structures. Consistent with Blau's (1970) formulation, Langworthy viewed spatial, occupational, hierarchical, and functional differentiation as the structural core of police organizations. Maguire's (2003) study of the determinants of police organizational structure also stressed the importance of spatial, hierarchical or vertical, and functional differentiation, while also including centralization, formalization, and administrative density as core structural elements. Maguire (1997) also used all these elements except spatial differentiation to represent organizational structure. Zhao (1996) employed many of these same concepts in his study of police organizational change, though also adding managerial tenure and personnel diversity as core structural elements. Wilson (2003) was the only one to utilize professionalism (among the other common measures just discussed) as an element of structure.

Structural Complexity and Control

Organizational structure is often considered in terms of complexity and control. Structural complexity refers to differentiation within the organization. Hall, Johnson, and Haas (1967, p. 906) define it as "the degree of internal segmentation — the number of separate 'parts' of the organization as reflected by the division of labor, number of hierarchical levels, and the spatial dispersion of the organizations." Hall (1972) argues the three most common elements of complexity are spatial dispersion, vertical or hierarchical differentiation, and horizontal differentiation representing functional and occupational differentiation.

Structural control represents the mechanisms by which differentiation of the organization is managed or coordinated. This often occurs through centralization, formalization, administrative weight or density, and professionalism. Centralization helps to maintain control by relegating decision-making authority to those holding high-ranking positions in the organization (Child, 1973b). Formalization, as Hall (1972, p. 196) defines it, "is a means of prescribing how, when, and by whom tasks are to be performed." Hall, Johnson, and Haas (1967, p. 911) also define it as "a means of controlling the behavior of the members of the organization by limiting individual discretion" (see also Cordner, 1989). By defining the procedures by which work is to be completed, policies coordinate organization efforts. Ensuring an organization has a proper administrative weight or density (e.g., a proper ratio of administrative to production employees, or police line officers) helps improve coordination within an organization (Rushing, 1967). Professionalism can also help introduce control (Cordner; Hall et al.) and lead to a coordinating mechanism with authority derived from knowledge and skill (Rushing). As Blau, Heydebrand, and Stauffer (1966) suggest, professional qualifications contribute to coordination by permitting employees to see the implications of their work and place it in a larger context.

Rushing's (1967) "differentiation-coordination" hypothesis, stemming from Durkheim's (1933) work on the division of labor, suggests that the more complex a social unit becomes, the greater need it has for internal coordination. Blau (1970) recognized this in suggesting that structural differentiation enhances the administrative component of an organization because coordination and communication demand administrative attention. He confirmed in his study of employment agencies that both vertical and horizontal differentiation were positively related to the proportion of supervisors and administrative staff to total personnel.

There have been two rigorous examinations of the relationship between structural complexity and control in large municipal police organizations. Maguire (2003) analyzed spatial, vertical, and functional differentiation as variables of complexity and centralization, formalization, and administrative density as variables of control in the 432 largest U.S. municipal police organizations. He found no relationship between structural complexity and control; not one measure of structural complexity was statistically related to any of the three measures of structural control. Though convincing, these findings should not be deemed conclusive because they are based on a single test. In addition, Maguire estimated his models independently rather than in a system, estimating equations one at a time. Though this helps reduce specification error and increases statistical power, it minimizes the extent to which the full information of the larger model can be used to estimate its parameters.

Wilson (2003) also examined the differentiation-coordination hypothesis in the context of police organizations. His multiple-indicator-multiple-cause (MIMIC) model treated structural control as a latent construct (i.e., an unmeasured variable estimated from directly observed variables) measured by centralization, formalization, administrative weight, and elements of professionalism in a sample of 401 large U.S. municipal police organizations. Unlike Maguire (2003), he found occupational and functional differentiation positively associated with structural control. He also found spatial and hierarchical differentiation unrelated to structural control. This provides some evidence supporting the relationship between structural complexity and control in police organizations. This study did not, however, control for other factors such as the effects of organizational context on structural control. It would be useful to retest these relationships on different samples, using a full-estimation procedure that assesses all the relationships simultaneously, and accounting for various determinants of organizational structure.

Criticisms of Organizational Structure Studies

Research on organizational structure could benefit from improved measurement. Most studies specify concepts represented by a single measure, with multiple measures, where they exist, treated independently. For example, Langworthy (1986) used the number of day beats, night beats, and precinct stations to indicate spatial differentiation. Though using these three measures is better than using only one, this particular strategy suffered from an inability to statistically pool information from all measures to represent the construct of interest. Structural equation models would permit such enhanced measurement while simultaneously offering an interval-level estimate of the construct and statistical predictions of how well the measures represent it.

Like Langworthy, Maguire (2003) used the number of police beats and facilities as indicators of spatial differentiation. Through structural equation modeling, he was able to treat spatial differentiation as an unobserved latent construct, and use the number of police beats and facilities as simultaneous measures of this construct. These types of factor-analytic measurement techniques represent a significant advancement in the study of police organizations.[4] Nevertheless, further improvements, as in all research, remain possible.

Prescription of Structural Role in Community Policing

Several researchers acknowledge that changes in the police organizational structure must accompany COP implementation. Nevertheless, the causal order of the association between organizational structure and COP implementation is not clear. Although discussion of this topic often seems to imply structural transformation must precede COP, some researchers argue organizational changes and community-oriented activities must occur coincidentally.

Wilkinson and Rosenbaum (1994) address this question of causality in their study of the Aurora and Joliet (Illinois) police agencies. They found little evidence that the implementation of problem-solving efforts affected organizational structure. Rather, they concluded that organizations with bureaucratic, hierarchical, and centralized structures would find it difficult to develop an environment to facilitate COP and other problem-solving efforts. That is, implementation of problem-solving efforts did not influence organizational structure, but organizational structure affected the implementation of problem-solving efforts. For example, the Aurora department implemented a formal paperwork system to encourage the involvement of the entire department in problem-solving efforts, but the structure of the department was such that the effort soon focused on the documentation process rather than actual problem-solving efforts.

Wilson and Donnermeyer (2002) found a similar effect in their study of crossfunctional problem-solving teams in the Columbus (Ohio) Division of Police. While the documentation and team meeting process were designed to enhance communication and collaboration among various functional units, many officers felt the formalized process impeded actual problem-solving efforts.

To facilitate COP, Sparrow (1998) claims police organizations should reduce hierarchy and formalization and decentralize decision-making, shifting it to geographical areas and individual officers. He claims current mechanistic police structures hinder the ideals of COP, so the headquarters of the organization should communicate in detail the basic values and objectives of the organization and encourage district stations and individual officers to use their discretion in specific situations. Rosenbaum concurs, suggesting the quasi-military structures of

American police agencies are a major obstacle to the implementation of COP, and that they should be geographically based, flattened, and decentralized (Tafoya, 1997).

Goldstein (1990) explains many police agencies devote considerable resources to responding to calls for service but do not typically seek to solve community problems through their own initiative. To improve policing, he suggests policies and organizational structure be modified to accommodate and support organizational change. Skolnick and Bayley (1986) suggest civilianization of police organizations boosts community-oriented efforts by alleviating sworn officers from the pressures of the 911 system (e.g., civilians can perform support tasks, which frees sworn officers and allows them to be in the community) and drawing on civilians with specialized linguistic and cultural skills. Skolnick and Bayley find decentralization necessary but not sufficient to develop direct relationships between the police and the community.

Greene, Bergman, and McLaughlin (1994, p. 93) consider the role of organizational structure in COP implementation more generally, writing

> For community policing to become a central feature of American law enforcement, the institutional framework and organizational apparatus of police organizations must be altered . . . to accommodate . . . sweeping changes. The success or failure of community policing [is] affected by the organizational structures and processes that characterize modern-day policing.

Riechers and Roberg (1990, p. 111) concur with this assessment, warning

> If changes in police organization, management, and personnel are not forthcoming, as the police role continues to become more complex, community policing could turn out not only to be a failure, but actually dangerous to the requirements of policing a democratic society.

Because the paramilitary structure of American police agencies may smother innovation and creativity (Bayley, 1988), COP requires police organizations to move away from a mechanistic, centralized structural orientation to a more open, organic, and decentralized structure (Greene, 2000; Kuykendall and Roberg, 1982; Roberg, 1994).

Evidence of Structural Role

Though researchers consistently prescribe structural changes for COP implementation, there is little evidence such change is undertaken before COP implementation (Greene, 2000; Mastrofski, 1998). Weisel and Eck (1994, p. 95), in a study of COP initiatives in six cities, found "none of the agencies were directly involved in formal decentralization by flattening their organizations." Though this finding confuses the organizational concepts of centralization (i.e., point of decision-making) and hierarchical differentiation (i.e., extent of a rank structure), the point remains that formal reduction of the organizational hierarchy did not occur in any of these cities.

Does this mean that, in practice, organizational structure has no relationship to COP, or that changes in organizational structure may facilitate COP implementation but are not necessary conditions? The answer is not entirely clear. The empirical studies have not confirmed a relationship between organizational structure and COP. While some specific aspects of organizational structure may influence COP implementation, the effects of these have not been consistent across studies.

Maguire (1997) examined change in organizational structure over a six-year period among 236 police agencies that were not planning to implement COP, were planning to implement COP, or had implemented COP. Controlling for organization size and task scope (measured by an additive index of 17 primary responsibilities of the agency), he examined changes in five structural measures: organizational height, functional differentiation, civilianization, formalization, and administrative density. Civilianization, formalization, and administrative density did not change for these departments over the time he studied. Organizational height decreased, as was expected, but functional differentiation increased, which was not expected. Furthermore, there were no statistical differences on these variables by whether departments were not planning to implement COP, were planning to implement COP, or had implemented COP. One limitation of this research, which Maguire concedes, is that the validity of his categorization of agencies depends on the truthfulness of agencies' claims regarding COP implementation. He compares agencies by what they claim to do, not what they actually do. Some agencies claim to have COP but do not fulfill its requirements (Trojanowicz et al., 1998). The research in this book suffers from the same limitation, as do others that rely on survey data.

Zhao (1996) constructed measures of COP that differentiated between internally and externally focused change. Controlling for region and city size, he found the number of line officers as a percentage of all department personnel — a measure of hierarchical differentiation — was positively related to externally focused change, but had no statistically significant association with internally focused change. He found no association with either measure of change and the number of divisions and patrol beats (measures of spatial differentiation), civilians as a percentage of department personnel (a measure of occupational differentiation), and number of ranks (a measure of hierarchical differentiation).

King's (1998) investigation of innovation in American municipal police organizations yielded somewhat different results. As previously noted, his measures of COP included radical innovation, indicating whether an organization had both implemented COP and assigned officers to it, and programmatic innovation, indicating whether an organization had community crime prevention programs and foot patrols. He regressed these two measures on 33 variables representing organizational, ascriptive, and environmental aspects of each police organization. He found a positive impact of the number of patrol beats on radical but not programmatic innovation, and a positive impact of specialization on programmatic but not radical innovation. While controlling for city size and other community characteristics, he found no association between either measure of innovation and the number of stations and organizational structural characteristics such as height, segmentation, centralization, formalization, vertical concentration, and administrative overhead.

Reasons for Further Investigation

The extant empirical studies suggest organizational structure matters very little in COP implementation. Nevertheless, there are at least three reasons to investigate this issue further.

First, there is the issue of implementation measurement. To find if structure is related to COP, it is necessary to have good measures of both constructs. Maguire's (1997) and King's (1998) studies rely on organizational claims regarding COP implementation that may not resemble actual implementation activities. Both studies use a dichotomous or ordinal measure of implementation, neither of which are as precise as an interval-level measure would be. Zhao (1996) seeks to overcome the measurement problem with the use of a twelve-item external and six-item internal scale. Because this approach combines more information and has a greater range, it is more sensitive than a dichotomous or ordinal measure with few categories, and is superior to any measure based upon a single item. Nevertheless, these scales of implementation are not interval-based because they are truncated at the low and high ends of the continuum, and because the distance between categories may not be equal. Furthermore, they do not account for measurement error, which Maguire and Uchida (2000) contend may be a critical issue, but is generally overlooked in police research. These shortcomings may help account for the lack of association or unexpected relationships among measures. In short, there cannot be a definitive conclusion about the relationship between organizational structure and COP until improved measurements of constructs are created and used.

Second, organizational changes are part of the COP philosophy. Scholars have argued that attuning police organizations to this philosophy will require changes in police organization, management, and structure (e.g., Greene et al., 1994; Riechers and Roberg, 1990, Tafoya, 1997). Given the philosophical association between COP implementation and organizational structure and the empirical evidence that COP has not influenced police organization structure (e.g., Maguire, 1997), it is critical to empirically account for the impact of structure on COP implementation. This is especially true given some evidence (e.g., King, 1998; Zhao, 1996) that organizational structure determines COP change and innovation.

The third reason to further examine organizational structure and COP is the findings of the innovation literature. COP is often described as a form of police innovation (King, 1998 and 2000; Skolnick and Bayley, 1986; Zhao, 1996). If COP is indeed an organizational innovation, then those variables that facilitate or impede its implementation should be similar to those that do the same for other organizational innovations. Daft (1982) summarizes the consensus that organic organizations are more innovative than more bureaucratic ones. Damanpour's (1991) analysis of twenty-three empirical studies on organizational innovation found specialization, functional differentiation, administrative density, professionalism, managerial attitude toward change, technical knowledge resources, slack resources (a measure of the difference between income and expenditure), and external and internal communication all positively affected innovation, while centralization affected it negatively.

Other scholars have examined additional details of organizational structure and innovation. Wilson (1966) theorized that the same organizational aspects (e.g., diversity) that support the idea of innovation impede its adoption. Duncan (1976) noted organizations needed to be "ambidextrous" to innovate, given that organic structures better facilitate the initiation of innovation and creative ideas, but mechanistic structures are better able to implement them.

Scholars have differentiated between types of innovation. Damanpour (1987) differentiated the innovations of seventy-five public libraries into three types: technological, administrative, and ancillary. He found that specialization and organizational slack were positively related to technological innovations, but not associated with administrative or ancillary innovations. Administrative intensity was positively correlated with technological and administrative, but not ancillary, innovation. Organization size was positively associated only with administrative innovations.[5] Damanpour found no significant relationship between functional differentiation and type of innovation.

Ettlie, Bridges, and O'Keefe (1984) examined the association between innovation for new products, radical process, and incremental process and organizational complexity, centralization, and formalization in a study of meat, canning, and fish industries. Like Damanpour (1991), they confirmed centralization was negatively related to innovation. Unlike Damanpour, they found formalization to be positively related to all types of innovation. They also found a positive relationship between organizational complexity and all three types of innovation.

Their findings, however, are based on correlation analysis and consequently do not simultaneously estimate all the effects while controlling for others.

Daft (1982) made an additional distinction by considering the administrative and technical cores of organizations. He suggested an organic administrative core and a mechanistic technical core are appropriate for administrative innovations, while a mechanistic administrative core and an organic technical core are appropriate for technical innovations.

There is evidence that different types of police innovation exist as well. King (2000) examined innovation in the 431 largest U.S. municipal police agencies. His exploratory factor analysis determined that although the exact number of dimensions could not be determined, police innovation is a multidimensional concept. Certain types of police innovation may be more or less associated with organizational structure than others.

6

ORGANIZATIONAL CONTEXT AND ORGANIZATIONAL STRUCTURE

The organizational context for police organizations includes both task and institutional environments. These environments comprise elements to which police respond in efforts to maximize organizational effectiveness and improve perceived legitimacy. This chapter identifies specific elements encompassed in the context of police organizations and their relationship with organizational structure.

Task Environment

Organization Size

Among those who have explored the issue of organization size and structure of large police agencies are Langworthy (1986), Maguire (2003), and King (1999).

Langworthy's correlation analyses of data originally gathered by Ostrom (1979) on 106 police organizations and by the Kansas City (Missouri) Police Department on 69 jurisdictions found only modest relationships between size and hierarchy (number of layers, height of the hierarchy, and concentration in lower ranks) and to functional differentiation (task specialization). He also found a modest inverse relationship between size and occupational differentiation (measured by civilianization), a somewhat large positive correlation between size and spatial differentiation (measured by the number of police stations and beats), and a negative relationship between size and the proportion of officers ranking sergeant and above but a positive relationship between size and the proportion of officers assigned to administration.

Maguire extended Langworthy's analysis with path models exploring the relationship between size and organizational structure. Controlling for the influence of other organizational variables (e.g., organization age, task scope and routineness, environmental capacity, dispersion, instability), and using improved measures of spatial and vertical differentiation derived from confirmatory factor analyses, he found organization size to be positively related to all measures of structural complexity (i.e., spatial, vertical, and functional differentiation) and (controlling for structural complexity as well) statistically unassociated with all measures of structural control (i.e., centralization, formalization, and administration).

Controlling for organization age, King also found organization size to be positively associated with civilianization (i.e., occupational differentiation), hierarchical height, and functional differentiation. Unlike Maguire, he found larger organizations were more formalized, an indication of structural control. According to his study, size was not associated with the percent of full-time staff devoted to administrative duties.

In summary, the size of the organization appears to exhibit a fairly consistent impact on structural complexity, but its impact on structural control is not consistent across studies. Further research will help to clarify the relationship between size and structural control.

Organization Age

Downs (1967) contends organizational structure is a function of concentrations of like employees that change over time, resulting in organizations that become more conservative with age. This, he claims, also results in organizations becoming more functionally differentiated and relying to a greater extent on administration and formalization as they age. However, this effect may be less applicable to police organizations, which are generally much older than the organizations Downs considered. However, the experience that comes with age may affect organizational structure if (1) the agencies learn under what conditions and for what purposes various forms of structure are most effective, and (2) they adjust their organizations based on this knowledge. King (1999) and Maguire (2003) have explored the effect of age on police organizations. Controlling for organization size, King found that organization age was negatively related to civilianization — that is, older organizations were less occupationally differentiated. King found no impact of age on hierarchical height, functional differentiation, formalization, or administration of police organizations. Maguire also found age was unassociated with functional differentiation, centralization, formalization, and administration. Contrary to King, he did find a statistically significant positive influence of age on vertical differentiation and a nearly significant association ($p < 0.10$) between age and spatial differentiation.

Task Scope

Perrow's (1967) conception of routine technologies coincides with mechanistic structures and processes (i.e., spatially concentrated, differentiated occupationally and functionally, and hierarchically tall), whereas nonroutine technologies are associated with organic structures and processes (i.e., geographically dispersed, little occupational and functional differentiation, and flattened hierarchies). Thompson (1967, p. 78) finds "no 'one best way' to structure complex organizations," but rather that organizations handle contingencies by developing elaborate structural responses. In other words, the more task demands are placed on an organization, the more the organization will guard its integrity through control over the variables it can manage.[1]

Langworthy (1986) applied Perrow's (1967) framework to Wilson's (1968) study of police behavior. He found use of nonroutine technology indicated a "team" style of policing while use of routine technology indicated a "legalistic" style. He concluded (pp. 95–96) that "agency size . . . explains spatial differentiation, and technology largely accounts for functional differentiation. Hierarchical differentiation, occupational differentiation, and administrative overhead . . . appear relatively independent or, at most, weakly related to size and technology." Langworthy acknowledged his measure of routineness — or, as he labeled it, standardization, based on the proportion of operation employees not assigned to patrol — reflected organizational structure rather than technology; nevertheless, he suggests it is an adequate global measure of operational methodology, as it indicates the extent to which resources are not devoted to a production method known to be nonstandard.

In addition to noting its focus on structure rather than technology, Maguire (2003) criticized Langworthy's measure for being substantively uninformative because it says little about what police do. He attempted to improve upon Langworthy's measure by developing a (non)routineness index comprising eleven measures related to COP. Here COP is considered to be a nonroutine technology, a way of transforming inputs into outputs by working with the community as a coproduction network. In addition to task routineness, Maguire contends task scope is another dimension of technology.[2] Maguire treated task routineness and scope as distinct measures of technology, both of which could influence police organizations. Though earlier work (e.g., Child, 1973a; Harvey, 1968; Hsu et al., 1983; Perrow, 1967; Woodward, 1965) linked technology and organizational structure, Maguire's path models found little impact of technology on police organizational structure. Among his structural complexity (centralization, formalization, administration) and control (vertical, functional, and spatial differentiation) measures, he found only task routineness to determine functional differentiation. Contrary to Perrow's (1967) expectations but consistent with those of Thompson (1967), Maguire found a greater reliance on nonroutine technology was associated with higher levels of functional differentiation. He found no significant effect of task scope on any of the complexity and control measures.[3]

Based on these two studies, technology influences functional differentiation, a form of structural complexity, in terms of task routineness. Task scope or variability does not appear related to organizational structure, but only one study tested this relationship. Given the importance of this variable to Perrow's (1967) influential typology, it would be useful to confirm this relationship does not apply to police organizations in another examination.

Community Characteristics

Most studies exploring community uncertainty and police organizational structure tend to find small or inconsistent associations between them. Langworthy (1986, p. 109) concluded, "There appears to be no significant degree of determinism operating between population, mobility, complexity, and police organizational structure." Nonetheless, he did uncover some small but significant correlations between his environmental and structural measures, with population change related to occupational differentiation, two of four measures of hierarchical differentiation, and one of four measures of administrative overhead; industrial heterogeneity associated with two of three measures of spatial differentiation, occupational differentiation, three of four measures of hierarchical differentiation, and both measures of functional differentiation; and occupational heterogeneity correlated with three of four measures of hierarchical differentiation and one of two measures of functional differentiation. He also found his environmental measures explained about a third of the variation in occupational differentiation. Such findings provide at least modest evidence supporting a relationship between community uncertainty and police organizational structure.

Maguire (2003) developed a measurement model of environmental complexity using heterogeneity in income, race, and education as indicators. His path analysis found no statistical relationship between these indicators and his measures of structural complexity and control. He did find a positive association between environmental uncertainty, represented by police chief turnover, and spatial differentiation. This led him to conclude the most important question pertaining to uncertainty is whether it penetrates organizational boundaries, though he also conceded the measure of environmental uncertainty was not ideal.

Community characteristics appear to be associated with structural complexity and control, but the relationship depends on how the constructs are measured. Additional study will help elucidate the extent to which community characteristics determine how the police structure their organizations.

Institutional Environment

Environmental Capacity

Maguire (2003) found no relationship between environmental capacity and structural complexity or control. McCabe and Fajardo (2001), however, found structural differences between accredited and non-accredited law enforcement agencies. Accredited agencies were more likely to operate drug and child abuse units (indicating greater functional differentiation), and to require drug testing for sworn applicants, more field training hours, and a higher level of minimum education for new officers (indicating greater professionalism). Methodological limitations, however, require that the findings of this analysis be interpreted cautiously. McCabe and Fajardo provided little information regarding the process and outcome of matching accredited and nonaccredited agencies. In addition, they differentiated police organizations as to their accreditation status in 1998, but examined organizational differences from the 1993 Law Enforcement Management and Administrative Statistics survey. As the authors contend, hundreds of police organizations apply for accreditation each year. Consequently, it is possible that agencies considered accredited for the study actually were not accredited in 1993, and vice versa. Therefore, it is important to review this relationship further.

Funding Incentives

To the extent that funding sources require (e.g., as a contractual obligation) or expect specific structural changes as part of the COP implementation process, we may expect the availability of COP funding to influence the structure of police agencies. This phenomenon would be consistent with both institutional and resource dependency theories. I investigate in this book the previously unexamined hypothesis that the amount of COP funding influences the structure of police organizations.

Region

Previous empirical research has not explored in any critical way if and how police organizational structures differ by region. It is likely the same institutional forces that lead to regional variation in COP activities lead to differences in police organizational structure.

7

MODELS, DATA, AND ANALYSIS

Conceptual Model

The primary objective of this book is to explore the determinants of COP implementation and its relationship with organizational structure. Previous research indicates the organizational context of police organizations may influence both their formal structures and community policing activities. Moreover, there may be a simultaneous relationship between organizational structure and COP implementation. These propositions form the conceptual model, depicted in Figure 7.1, that I test in this book. Because the measures and relationships I discuss are extensive, I encourage the reader to refer to this simple model frequently. It succinctly summarizes the basic foundation of this research.

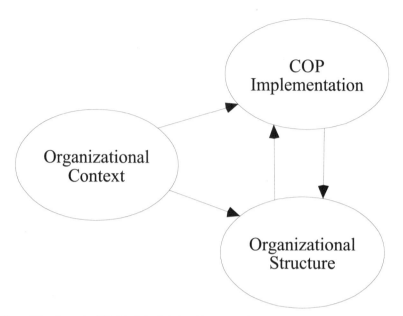

Figure 7.1   Conceptual Model of the Relationships among Organizational Context, Organizational Structure, and COP Implementation.

Data Sources

I gathered data to test the conceptual model from several sources. These included the 1997 and 1999 Law Enforcement Management and Administrative Statistics (LEMAS) surveys (Bureau of Justice Statistics, 1999 and 2000), the 1990 U.S. Census, surveys conducted by Maguire (2003) and King (1998), and grants data from COPS (2001).

LEMAS

The LEMAS surveys are a general administrative survey sponsored by the U.S. Bureau of Justice Statistics and conducted by the U.S. Census Bureau every two to three years. Both the 1997 and 1999 surveys were distributed to every municipal police organization listed in the Directory Survey of Law Enforcement Agencies with one hundred or more sworn full-time equivalent employees. These "large" municipal police agencies comprise the unit of analysis for my research. In 1997, 462 agencies participated in the survey, while 497 agencies participated in 1999.[1]

U.S. Census

The U.S. Census of 1990 offered much of the information needed to construct measures of organizational context. I used the 1990, rather than 2000, decennial census data for two reasons. First, Census 2000 city-level data were not available when I began this analysis. Second, if there are any causal-temporal order relationships between the organizational context, organizational structure, and COP implementation, the contextual factors would theoretically precede the other elements. Census 1990 data were the most recent available prior to the data regarding organizational structure. Edward Maguire kindly provided these data, which he had also used in earlier work (2003).

Maguire and King Surveys

Maguire (2003) surveyed the 432 largest U.S. municipal police organizations for organizational data in 1996. A total of 395 (91 percent) agencies responded to this survey. He asked agencies to provide information about their organization as of both 1993 and 1996. Many of the variables he collected were also those required for the present research, and he kindly provided these data as well. These data include 1994 accreditation status as obtained from the Commission on Accreditation for Law Enforcement Agencies. Neither his survey data nor accreditation data perfectly matched the 1997 LEMAS data in terms of the year in which the information represents. One of these variables, however — organization age — could be and was adjusted to 1997 values. The missing values of this variable were substituted from information King (1998) gathered in a survey he conducted in 1994. I, therefore, had to assume the characteristics other than organization age were indicative of what they would be in 1997, which is the year in which the first LEMAS wave provides information. This assumption is necessary to establish a common temporal period among the variables.

COPS

The COPS Office is responsible for distributing community policing grants to police agencies nationwide. As such, it possesses data on the amount of community policing funds granted to agencies. The COPS Office (2001) provided this information for this research.

Merged Sample

For a police organization to be included in this study, at least some information pertaining to the organization had to have been available from all the above sources. Merging the data from the above sources yielded 401 such organizations. These organizations comprise the sample that I analyze. Although this sample is nonrandom, it does represent about 80 percent of all large U.S. municipal police agencies.[2] For the majority of variables in this study, the data are complete for each organization. Where this was not the case, the maximum likelihood estimation process required these missing values to be imputed to create full data matrices. For each variable. I note if any values required imputation. Where imputation was necessary, I generally imputed the missing values with either the mean or mode of the variable depending on whether the variable is continuous. This form of imputation does not affect the point estimate (assuming the missing values are not systematic) of a specific variable, but can artificially increase the significance of the relationship it has with other variables. None of the few variables that had many missing variables exhibited relationships with other variables that were only slightly significant, so this potential bias does not appear to be substantively important in this study.

Unfortunately, like many similar studies, this research is limited by the nature of secondary data from organizational sources. As Maguire and Katz (2002) posit, persons completing such surveys may be careless, exaggerate, or even lie in their responses. They could be uninformed or misinformed about the activities of their organizations. Respondents may also have varying interpretations of the issues queried, meaning it is difficult to ascertain dosage through the data of such surveys. For example, what constitutes "COP training" or "formed problem-solving partnerships with the community" may vary by organization. This research must assume similarity in each organization's operational definition and implementation of these activities, an assumption that may not always be warranted. Finally, this research is limited to the measures available in the sources it uses. Although the measures available in these sources are indicative of major COP dimensions, there are not good measures for all potential dimensions. For example, the LEMAS measures do not provide good insight on organizational belief in a broad policing function (beyond engagement of problem-solving) or decentralized decision making. Therefore, this book cannot be considered to be an exhaustive analysis of COP activities, but only of those for which there are reliable data. Future research should explore the models developed herein using larger item pools of community policing and other measures.

Measures

Organizational Context

Previous research suggests elements of both the task and institutional environment form an organization's context, and that this context is important for understanding variability in COP implementation. The data sources I consider provide several measures of these components. Measures of task-related components available in these data include organization size and age, technology, and community characteristics. Measures of institution-related components available in these data include environmental capacity, funding incentives, and region. I describe below specific measures of organizational context. Table 7.1 offers descriptive statistics of these measures.

Organization Size. I measured organization size as the total number of sworn and nonsworn full-time equivalent employees. The LEMAS survey provided this information. Given the work of previous researchers (e.g., Blau, 1971; Child, 1973a; Maguire, 2003) who found nonlinear influences and skewness in this variable, the variable was logged (i.e., like earlier researchers mentioned, I analyze the logarithmic values for this variable). The logged variable ranged from 4.70 to 10.79 and had a mean value of 5.84 (the raw size had a range of 110 to 48,487 and a mean of 712).

Organization Age. I acquired data on organization age from surveys by Maguire (2003) and King (1998), who calculated age as the estimated number of years since the organization began uniformed, paid, full-time twenty-four-hour police services.[3] The youngest organization was

Table 7.1   Descriptive Statistics of Observed Organizational Context and Structure Variables (n = 401)

	Data Year	Source	Minimum	Maximum	Mean	Std. Deviation
Organizational Context						
Organization Size (Ln)	1997	LEMAS	4.7005	10.7891	5.8381	0.8746
Organization Age	1997	Maguire/ King	17.0000	163.0000	98.9015	32.6650
Task Scope	1997	LEMAS	10.0000	24.0000	17.2594	2.5461
Race Heterogeneity	1990	Census	0.0337	0.6744	0.3555	0.1591
Income Heterogeneity	1990	Census	0.8076	0.8804	0.8556	0.0110
Unemployed (%)	1990	Census	2.3766	19.6669	7.0431	2.7022
Police Chief Turnover	1993	Maguire	1.0000	13.0000	4.3491	1.7082
Population Mobility (%)	1990	Census	28.6957	72.5649	50.9836	8.3315
Environmental Capacity	1997	LEMAS/ Maguire	0.0000	4.0000	1.7855	0.7993
Funding Incentive*	1997	COPS	0.0000	46.9762	3.2866	3.6754
Western Region	n/a	Census	0.0000	1.0000	0.2344	0.4242
Organizational Structure 1997						
Stations	1997	LEMAS	1.0000	216.0000	7.9526	15.2819
Occupational Differentiation	1997	LEMAS	0.0000	0.5000	0.3721	0.0978
Ranks	1993	Maguire	4.0000	12.0000	6.0175	0.9446
Functional Units	1997	LEMAS	0.0000	16.0000	7.8853	3.2484
Centralization	1993	Maguire	21.0000	77.0000	53.2807	8.3253
Formalization	1997	LEMAS	3.0000	10.0000	8.4813	1.3078
Administrative Weight	1997	LEMAS	3.2432	51.2000	24.7963	7.4824
Organizational Structure 1999						
Stations	1999	LEMAS	1.0000	266.0000	8.2843	17.1595
Occupational Differentiation	1999	LEMAS	0.0341	0.5000	0.3818	0.0892
Formalization	1999	LEMAS	5.0000	10.0000	8.7556	1.1896
Administrative Weight	1999	LEMAS	6.1538	56.0554	25.3213	7.5419

* Per full-time equivalent employee and measured in 1,000s.

estimated to be 17 years old, whereas the oldest was 163 years.[4] On average, these agencies aged 98.9 years old.

Task Scope. The LEMAS survey asked respondents to indicate up to twenty-nine functions for which their organizations had primary responsibility.[5] Similar to that constructed by Maguire (2003) and King (1998), I constructed a scale of task scope by adding the number of functions for which the organization maintained primary responsibility. Agencies reported having primary responsibility from 10 to 24 tasks and an average of 17.26 tasks.

Population Complexity. The 1990 Census includes data on five race categories and nine income categories. As a measure of population complexity, I calculated the heterogeneity within each complexity type using the Gibbs-Martin D, a measure of differentiation, or heterogeneity, among the number of categories within it.[6] Based on this measure of differentiation, the least possible amount of heterogeneity, zero, occurs when all persons are in only one category. The maximum possible amount of differentiation for race is 0.80, occurring when a population is equally distributed among the five race categories, and the maximum possible amount of differentiation for income is 0.89, when a population is equally distributed among the nine income categories. Race heterogeneity for the jurisdictions ranged from 0.03 to 0.67 with a mean value of 0.36; income heterogeneity ranged from 0.81 to 0.88 with an average of 0.86.

Socioeconomic Status. I use proportion of residents in the 1990 Census who were in the labor force but not employed as a measure of socioeconomic status. Among these jurisdictions, this ranged from 2.38 percent to 19.67 percent, with an average value of 7.04 percent.

Police Chief Turnover. I acquired data on police chief turnover from a survey by Maguire (2003), who asked each organization its number of chiefs from 1970 to 1993. The organizations reported their number of police chiefs ranged from one to thirteen, with an average of 4.35.[7]

Population Mobility. I use the proportion of residents at least five years old in the 1990 Census who lived at a different address in 1985 as a measure of population mobility. By this measure, mobility ranged from 28.70 percent to 72.56 percent, with an average value of 50.98 percent.

Environmental Capacity. I created an index of four potential external influences to measure environmental capacity. The first was whether the organization had both collective bargaining processes and a collective bargaining association (e.g., police union, nonpolice union, or police association). The second was the existence of a civilian review board that reviews excessive force complaints. LEMAS data include variables on these first two constructs. The third was accreditation status as of January 1994 and gathered by Maguire (2003) from the Commission on Accreditation of Law Enforcement agencies. The fourth, also gathered by Maguire, was whether officers were hired through civil service.[8] Summing these four items created a scale ranging from 0 (for none of the external influences) to 4 (for all of them). Overall, 21 agencies were scored as having none of these influences, 112 reported one, 205 reported two, 58 reported three, and 5 reported four, yielding a mean score of 1.79.

Funding Incentives. The COPS Office has data on funds awarded for community policing. I used this information to calculate the total amount of COPS funding each agency had received as of June 30, 1997, and divided by the number of employees (organization size) to obtain a standardized measure of funding influence. Funding per employee ranged from zero to $44,976.22, with a mean value of $3,286.60.

Region. I constructed a dichotomous variable to identify organizations in the West as defined by the U.S. Census Bureau. Police agencies in the West are considered to be more innovative than those in other regions (Maguire et al., 1997; Zhao, 1996); this variable offered a means of testing this assertion in the model equations. Of the police organizations I analyze, 94, or 23 percent are in the West; the remaining 307 are elsewhere.

Structural Complexity

Information regarding four types of structural complexity was available in the data sources. These include spatial, occupational, hierarchical, and functional differentiation. I discuss the measures for each of these below. Descriptive statistics for each are summarized in Table 7.1.

Spatial Differentiation. I measured spatial differentiation by the number of facilities or stations listed in the LEMAS data. In addition to headquarters, this includes district or precinct stations, fixed and mobile neighborhood or community substations, and "other" facilities. Organizations ranged from 1 to 216 stations in 1997, with an average of 7.95, and from 1 to 266 in 1999, with an average of 8.28. The New York City Police Department increased its number of stations by fifty over this brief time period and represents the high end of the ranges in both years. Thirty-five organizations reported having one station in 1997, while 41 did so in 1999.

Occupational Differentiation. The LEMAS surveys contained data regarding the number of sworn and nonsworn full-time and part-time employees. I used this information to calculate a measure of occupational differentiation based on the Gibbs-Martin D formula. Because there were two categories of this variable, total sworn and total nonsworn, the maximum possible value of occupational differentiation is 0.5, occurring when an agency had an equal number of sworn and nonsworn employees. The range in this score for both 1997 and 1999 was zero to 0.5; the mean value was 0.37 in 1997 and 0.38 in 1999.[9]

Hierarchical Differentiation. The Maguire (2003) data provide the number of ranks within the organizational structure of the agency. The organization with the fewest ranks had four, while that with the highest had twelve. On average, organizations had about six distinct ranks.[10] This variable is available for 1993 only.

Functional Differentiation. The 1997 LEMAS survey asked organizations if they had one or more full-time employees in any of seventeen special units listed in the questionnaire.[11] I created an additive index representing the number of units each organization claimed to operate. Organizations scored from 0 to 16, with a mean of 7.89. These data were not available in 1999.

Structural Control

The data sources I used contained enough information to form three measures of structural control: centralization, formalization, and administrative weight. I discuss each of these below. Table 7.1 on page 60 lists descriptive statistics of these variables.

Centralization. Maguire (2003) developed an index of centralization based on responses to ten questions pertaining to decision-making by senior management and ten questions pertaining to decision-making by front-line supervisors.[12] Each question had a response category ranging from 0 to 4, with higher values indicating greater levels of centralization. Summing the responses to these twenty questions yields a scale from 0 to 80.[13] Observed values of this index ranged from 21 to 77, and had a mean of 53.28.[14] Data for this variable is available only for 1993.

Formalization. The LEMAS surveys ask each organization whether it has a written policy for ten different topics.[15] I created an index of formalization by summing the number of policy directives each organization had written. The number of written policy directives for each organization ranged from 3 to 10 in 1997 and from 5 to 10 in 1999, with an average of 8.48 in 1997 and 8.76 in 1999.

Administrative Weight. The LEMAS data contained information allowing the calculation of the administrative weight for each organization. I defined administrative weight as the proportion of total full-time employees (both sworn and nonsworn) assigned to administrative and technical support tasks. Administrative weight scores varied from 3.24 percent to 51.20 percent with a mean of 24.80 in 1997, and from 6.15 to 56.06 in 1999 with a mean of 25.32.[16]

Community Policing Implementation

The LEMAS surveys contained information regarding many activities generally associated with COP. These included variables pertaining to employee training, planning, fixed geographic assignment, problem-solving, and police–citizen interaction. For the purposes of this study, these represent five dimensions of community policing, and the extent of these activities ultimately represents the extent of community policing implementation. Some of these dimensions coincide with those identified by Maguire and Mastrofski's (2000) exploratory research on the community policing dimensions, such as training citizens and patrol officer activities, but not all. Instead, for this analysis I let the theory and discourse on community policing suggest the initial dimensions (subject to data limitations, of course) for empirical testing. For example, Maguire and Mastrofski identified a dimension pertaining to organizational structure, which I did not include as a measure of COP because I hypothesize that there may be a substantive relationship between organizational structure and COP implementation. I discuss each of the dimensions below. Table 7.2 on page 65 provides descriptive statistics for these measures.

Table 7.2 Descriptive Statistics of Observed Variables Used to Measure COP Implementation in 1997 (n = 462) and 1999 (n = 497)

	Data Year	Source	Range	Mean	Std. Deviation
Community Policing 1997					
COP Training					
Recruit COP Training	1997	LEMAS	0–3	2.5346	0.9978
Sworn COP Training	1997	LEMAS	0–3	1.9913	1.0435
Nonsworn COP Training	1997	LEMAS	0–3	0.9719	1.1128
Written COP Plan	1997	LEMAS	0–1	0.6126	0.4877
Fixed Assignment	1997	LEMAS	0–2	1.3074	0.6255
Problem-Solving	1997	LEMAS	0–3	1.6320	1.0512
Citizen Interaction					
Citizen COP Training	1997	LEMAS	0–1	0.6900	0.4610
Group Meetings	1997	LEMAS	0–8	5.4892	1.7185
Website	1997	LEMAS	0–1	0.4978	0.5005
Data Accessibility	1997	LEMAS	0–7	2.2100	1.8305
Community Policing 1999					
COP Training					
Recruit COP Training	1999	LEMAS	0–3	2.5996	0.8995
Sworn COP Training	1999	LEMAS	0–3	1.9115	1.0319
Nonsworn COP Training	1999	LEMAS	0–3	0.9879	1.0491
Written COP Plan	1999	LEMAS	0–1	0.6056	0.4892
Fixed Assignment	1999	LEMAS	0–2	1.4004	0.5738
Problem-Solving	1999	LEMAS	0–3	1.6962	1.0522
Citizen Interaction					
Citizen COP Training	1999	LEMAS	0–1	0.7500	0.4320
Group Meetings	1999	LEMAS	0–8	6.3300	1.8996
Website	1999	LEMAS	0–1	0.7082	0.4550
Data Accessibility	1999	LEMAS	0–8	3.7887	1.9514

Community Policing Training. The LEMAS data contain three measures of COP training. Agencies reported the proportion of new officer recruits, in-service sworn personnel, and civilian personnel who received at least eight hours of COP training during the previous three years. For each of the three types of personnel, agencies could respond none, less than half, more than half, or all. These responses are considered on a four-point scale ranging from 0 (none) to 3 (all).

Written Community Policing Plan. The second concept used to gauge COP implementation was whether the police organization had formally written a COP plan. Those that maintained written plans, coded as 1 on this dichotomous variable, were considered to be more serious about COP implementation than those who had not, coded as 0.

Fixed Geographic Assignment. The LEMAS survey contained two questions pertaining to fixed geographic assignment during the previous year. One was whether patrol officers were given responsibility for specific geographic areas or beats; the other was whether detectives were assigned to cases based on these geographic divisions. Organizations were coded 0 if neither function was geographically assigned, 1 if one but not both of these functions was assigned, and 2 if both were assigned.

Problem-Solving. The LEMAS survey asked organizations whether in the last year they (1) actively encouraged patrol officers to engage in SARA-type problem-solving projects on their beats (SARA stands for scanning, analysis, response, assessment), (2) included collaborative problem-solving projects in the evaluation criteria of patrol officers, and (3) formed problem-solving partnerships with community groups, municipal agencies, or others through specialized contracts or written agreements. Summing these three dichotomous variables, each scored as 0 or 1, yielded a scale ranging from 0 to 3 and varying by how many of these problem-solving activities the organization carried out.

Citizen Interaction. The LEMAS surveys include data on four measures of citizen interactions. The first is whether the police organization trained citizens in COP during the previous year. The second was whether the police organization maintained an official website. The third was whether the police held regular meetings in the previous year with eight specified types of groups.[17] The fourth was how the police shared information with the public through nine specified methods.[18] The first two variables were scored dichotomously, 0 for those doing so, 1 for those that did not. The other two were scored on additive indices, the third in a variable ranging from 0 to 8, the fourth in a variable ranging from 0 to 9.

Measurement Model

Much of the research on organizations and COP relies on single measures to represent complex constructs. This assumes that the variable perfectly represents the construct. Only recently has police scholarship used measurement models with multiple indicators for a single construct. Essentially, a measurement model provides a way to estimate an unmeasured, unobserved, or latent variable or construct based on pooling information from multiple directly measured or observed variables. Measurement models are superior to using a single variable for several reasons. First, information regarding several indicators — whether dichotomous, ordinal, or interval — instead of a single measure can be pooled to form a single estimate that is more precise. Second, the measurement error associated with each indicator can be assessed and controlled. Finally, several measures of model fit are available to assess how well the indicators represent the construct. I seek to develop a measurement model of COP implementation comprising many community-related activities.

Five COP-related activities, or dimensions, comprise the measures of COP implementation: training, written plan, fixed assignment, problem-solving, and citizen interaction. Two of these activities (training and citizen interaction), have multiple measures. Training is measured by its extent for recruit, sworn, and nonsworn personnel. Citizen interaction is measured by the proportion of citizens receiving COP training, the number of different types of community groups with which the police met, the existence of a website, and data accessibility.

Having multiple indicators for many of the concepts of interest permitted the construction of more sophisticated measures than would have been possible with only single indicators. I therefore treated these concepts as latent, unmeasured constructs that influenced the individual, directly observed variables. Together, several of the directly measured COP variables represent latent constructs that I in turn use to measure COP implementation.[19] This creates a higher-order measurement model of COP implementation. Thus, this research tests a second-order measurement model of COP implementation that ascertains whether a single latent factor (the second-order component of community policing implementation) determines both directly observed (community policing plan, fixed assignment, and problem-solving) and latent community policing dimensions (the first-order components of community policing training and citizen interaction). Figure 7.2 depicts the formal specification of this model.

Structural Model

The remaining directly measured variables — organization size and age, task scope, police chief turnover, population mobility, environmental capacity, funding incentives, region, stations, occupational differentiation, ranks, functional units, centralization, formalization, and administrative weight — combine with the measurement model to form the structural model to be tested. (As explained in Appendix A, the factor score of COP implementation is used for estimation of the structural model.) This model is a five-equation system that explains variation in

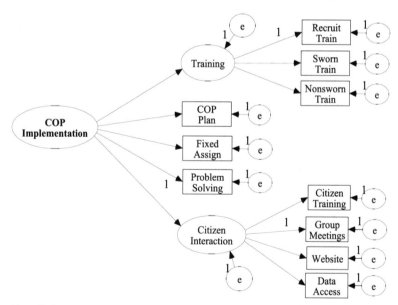

Note: Circles represent latent constructs, "e's" within a circle represents measurement error, and rectangles represent directly observed variables.

Figure 7.2   Measurement Model of COP Implementation.

structural complexity (i.e., stations and occupational differentiation) in 1999, structural control (i.e., formalization and administrative weight) in 1999, and COP implementation in 1999. Figure 7.3 shows how the exogenous variables predict these five endogenous variables. Structural complexity and control in 1997 influences COP implementation in 1999, structural complexity in 1997 determines structural control in 1999, and community policing implementation in 1997 impacts structural complexity and control in 1999. Organizational context influences COP implementation and structural complexity and control in 1999. The model controls for previous COP implementation, number of stations, occupational differentiation, formalization, and administrative weight.

A significant benefit of this model is that it examines these relationships over time and is therefore more likely to illustrate causation than the commonly used cross-sectional sample based on a single point in time. However, the comprehensiveness of this model comes at a cost. Although this study represents nearly all large, municipal police organizations, this is a very complex model to test with a sample size of 401 police organizations because all the equations are estimated simultaneously. As such, the statistical power to detect findings is somewhat modest. Future research could retest this model by expanding the unit of analysis (e.g., include smaller municipal or county agencies), thereby increasing the sample size.

Confirmatory Factor and Path Analysis

To estimate and assess the COP measurement model and its latent constructs, I used confirmatory factor analysis (see Bollen, 1989). Once I determined the best fitting, most theoretically appropriate model using the 1997 LEMAS data, I retested the final specification simultaneously on the 1997 and 1999 waves of the LEMAS survey in a multigroup comparison analysis. I did this to determine whether the model fit was only a function of the 1997 LEMAS data (i.e., related to idiosyncratic features of the data) or could be validated with other data as well. The group analysis tested the following statistical hypotheses:

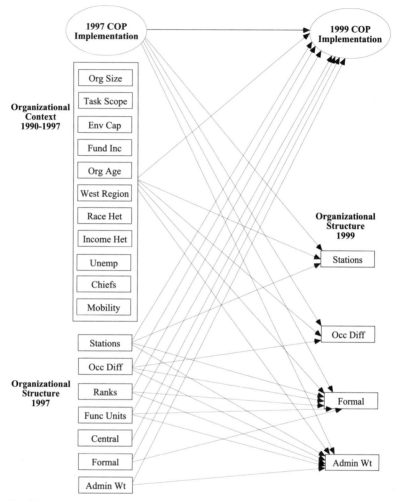

Note: Measurement errors and covariances among exogenous variables are not drawn to preserve space and clarity. Ovals represent variables derived from measurement models.

Figure 7.3   Structural Model of COP Implementation.

1. H_A: Form: the *dimensions and patterns* of factor loadings, measurement errors, and latent construct covariances are invariant (i.e., the form of the model not the actual estimates are invariant)

H_B: $\Lambda_X \Lambda_Y \Gamma$: the loadings of the measures on the latent constructs are invariant

H_C: $\Lambda_X \Lambda_Y \Gamma \Theta_\delta \Theta_\varepsilon$: the measurement error variances are invariant

H_D: $\Lambda_X \Lambda_Y \Gamma \Theta_\delta \Theta_\varepsilon \Phi \Psi$: the covariances of the latent constructs are invariant

As a final test of these additional constraints, I assessed the additional chi-square contribution of each successive constraint using the chi-square difference test. To be exhaustive, I tested all the remaining contrasts among the hypotheses.

To ensure proper estimation of the measurement models, I accounted for whether the data for each variable was dichotomous, ordinal, or interval in the estimation process. Most of the observed variables are ordinal or dichotomous. Bollen (1989) explains that inappropriately treating such variables as if they are continuous can adversely affect the chi-square fit statistic and tests of statistical significance, attenuate the standardized coefficient estimates, and cause correlation among the measurement errors. To account for differences in scale in my variables, I employed PRELIS (a statistical program to prepare data for structural analysis) to calculate the polyserial correlation matrix[20] and asymptotic covariance matrix for each model estimated. Using LISREL (a statistical program for structural analysis), I then weighted the polyserial correlation matrix by the asymptotic covariance matrix in a weighted least squares estimation of the model.

Path analyses are very similar to regression analyses in that all variables in the model are treated as though they are directly observed (i.e., there are no latent constructs). A path analysis takes on a much more general form than a regression analysis, however, because it can have multiple endogenous variables, thereby leading to more than one single equation. These systems of equations are often referred to as path models because they can easily be drawn to illustrate the direction of influence between variables in the model and all other components, thereby summarizing all equations in the model. For example, Figure 7.4, the path diagram,

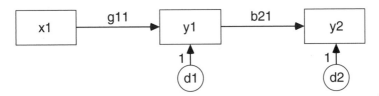

Figure 7.4   The path diagram.

illustrates that variable x_1 influences variable y_1, and the estimate of this impact is g_{11}. It further shows that y_1 impacts y_2, which is described by the coefficient b_{21}. The errors in equations are represented by d_1 and d_2. This diagram is therefore a visual depiction of the equations

$$y_1 = g_{11}x_1 + d_1$$

$$y_2 = b_{21}y_1 + d_2.$$

Bollen (1989) summarizes the general representation of these models as

$$y = B_y + \Gamma_x + \zeta$$

where y is a vector of endogenous variables, B is a coefficient matrix representing the endogenous on endogenous effects, x is a vector of exogenous variables, Γ is a coefficient matrix of the *exogenous* on endogenous impacts, and ζ is a vector representing the errors in equations.[21]

The variables described above permit testing the conceptual model, depicted in Figure 7.1, with the longitudinal structural model, depicted in Figure 7.3. This model will help delineate the determinants of COP implementation and the causal relationship between organizational structure and COP implementation. To explore the determinants of COP implementation, I test the effect of organizational context on COP implementation and organizational structure. To test the simultaneous relationship between organizational structure and COP implementation, I concurrently assess in the structural model (1) whether organizational structure in 1997 influences level of COP implementation in 1999 (while accounting for organizational context and previous level of COP implementation in 1997) and (2) whether the level of COP implementation in 1997 influences organizational structure in 1999 (while accounting for organizational context and previous organizational structure in 1997). This provides a more robust test of causality than a cross-sectional analysis of one point in time.

Both confirmatory factor analysis and path analysis are forms of structural equation modeling. Appendix A describes in more detail how I used confirmatory factor analysis for the measurement models in ways essentially identical to the way I analyzed the structural model using path analysis. Consistent with Bollen's (1989) procedures, for each model in both sets of analyses I specified the hypothesized relationships, determined the implied covariance matrix, ensured the model was globally identified, estimated the model using maximum likelihood, assessed the component and overall model fit, and respecified the model based on the initial findings only when warranted by theory.

8

FINDINGS

Conceptual Model

1997 Community Policing Measurement Model

Component Fit

The data sources offered multiple measures of COP training and citizen interaction, permitting two first-order latent constructs. These fit the data well. Table 8.1 shows the training (α = .001) and citizen interaction (α = .05) constructs were both statistically significant based on their construct variances and z-statistics. With recruit COP training and group meetings serving as a scale to their respective constructs,[1] all the measures were statistically significant at the $p<0.001$ level and, as expected, positive. Overall, the relationships between the measures and their corresponding constructs were strong. The weakest was that of data accessibility for citizen interaction, but even here the standardized factor loading, which indicates the strength and direction of the construct-measure relationship on a scale of −1 to 1, was 0.4235, significant at $p<0.001$, and the construct explained about 18 percent of the variance, as indicated by the R-square value.

Table 8.1   Estimates of the Second-Order COP Measurement Model, 1997

Component Fit	Standardized Factor Loadings	Z-ratio	R-square	Construct Variance	Z-ratio
First-Order					
COP Training				0.3414***	5.9530
Recruit COP Training[a]	0.8309		0.6903		
Sworn COP Training	0.9346***	15.4194	0.8735		
Nonsworn COP Training	0.7870***	17.1993	0.6194		
Citizen Interaction				0.0686*	2.2354
Citizen Training	0.7068***	8.3839	0.4995		
Group Meetings[a]	0.5342		0.2853		
Website	0.4547***	6.3903	0.2068		
Data Accessibility	0.4235***	7.2716	0.1794		
Second-Order					
COP Implementation				0.6428***	9.5641
COP Training	0.7110***	8.7791	0.5055		
Written COP Plan	0.5583***	9.1577	0.3117		
Fixed Assignment	0.4835***	9.2243	0.2338		
Problem-Solving[a]	0.8017		0.6428		
Citizen Interaction	0.8716***	7.9330	0.7597		
Model Fit					
$\chi^{2/\text{df}\,(p\text{-value})}$	59.3909/ 32 (0.0023)				
RMSEA	0.0431		IFI		0.9784
NFI	0.9543		Standardized RMR		0.0614
CFI	0.9782		AGFI		0.9827

[a] Served as the scale for the latent construct.
* $p<.05$, *** $p<.001$.

The second-order construct, COP implementation, was measured from the two first-order constructs (i.e., COP training and citizen interaction), and three directly measured variables (i.e., written COP plan, fixed assignment, and problem-solving). The construct was statistically significant at the $p<0.001$ level. As one might expect given the goals of COP, citizen interaction (a latent construct), with a standardized factor loading of 0.8716, and problem-solving (a directly measured variable), with a standardized factor loading of 0.8017, were most associated with the COP implementation construct. The values of their reliability statistics, 0.7597 for citizen interaction and 0.6428 for problem-solving, were also the highest among those for the COP implementation measures.

Overall Model Fit
The overall model fit also appears to be fairly good. Although the strict Chi-square text ($p=0.0023$) suggests the model does not fit the data perfectly, the Root Mean Square Error of Approximation (RMSEA), 0.0431, Normed Fit Index (NFI), 0.9543, Comparative Fit Index (CFI), 0.9782, Incremental Fit Index (IFI), 0.9784, Standardized Root Mean Square Residual (Standardized RMR), 0.0614, and Adjusted Goodness of Fit Index (AGFI), 0.9827, provide evidence of a good fitting model.[2] Given the overall component and model fit, I considered this specification satisfactory and tested it with multigroup analysis simultaneously using the 1997 and 1999 LEMAS data. A word of caution is necessary. A measurement model (or structural model) with good fit statistics does not necessarily mean it is the true representation of a construct or relationships. It simply means the model is consistent with the data. Other models may fit the data equally well (MacCallum, Wegener, Uchino, and Fabrigar, 1993). A useful model is therefore one that is both theoretically and empirically sound.

Measurement Model Comparison
This section provides the outcome of the process to compare and validate the measure of community policing implementation. Those less interested in the measurement process may wish to move on to the next section, which details the relationships among organizational context,

structure, and community policing as determined by the analysis of the structural model.

Hypothesis A

I first tested the hypothesis that the dimensions and patterns of factor loadings, measurement errors, and latent construct covariances are invariant across both waves of data.[3] The conservative Chi-square value was statistically significant (p=0.0001), suggesting that these items did vary across waves. Nevertheless, all other model fit measures indicated these items did not vary. The GFI (exceeding 0.99 for both years) and the standardized RMR (less than 0.07 in both years) suggested that each independent wave of data was consistent with the model. Furthermore, the RMSEA (0.0402), NFI (0.9520), CFI (0.9782), and IFI (0.9785) all indicated that, tested simultaneously, the model did not vary across waves. Overall, the findings appear to demonstrate that the dimensions and patterns of factor loadings, measurement errors, and latent construct covariances did not vary by wave. Table 8.2 provides the results of the invariance hypothesis tests.

Hypothesis B

In the second hypothesis, I added to Hypothesis A the constraint that the factor loadings of the measures of the latent constructs are invariant across waves. The model fit statistics of this more restrictive specification suggest that the factor loadings are invariant. The GFIs, both exceeding 0.98, and the Standardized RMRs, both less than 0.07, indicate the model fits each sample. The Chi-square value is significant (p<0.0001), but the remaining global fit measures — including RMSEA of 0.0420, NFI of 0.9431, CFI of 0.9729, and IFI of 0.9731 — all support the conclusion that the factor loadings are the same between the waves.

Table 8.3 shows the results of Chi-square difference tests for successive hypotheses. This test illustrated that adding the constraint of invariant factor loadings, Hypothesis B, to the constraints of invariant dimensions and patterns of factor loadings, measurement errors, and latent construct covariances significantly (p=0.0126) deteriorates the fit of the model. Although the fit may have appreciably decreased, the overall evidence suggests Hypothesis B may be consistent with both the 1997 and 1999 waves. The remaining contrasts in the table and

Table 8.2 Tests of Invariance of the COP Measurement Model, 1997 and 1999 Samples

| | Group Assessment | | | | | Global Assessment | | | |
| | GFI | | Standardized RMR | | | | | | |
Hypothesis	1997	1999	1997	1997	$\chi^{2}/\mathrm{df}\,(p\text{-value})$	RMSEA	NFI	CFI	IFI
H_A: Form	0.9900	0.9912	0.0614	0.0541	113.5411/64 (0.0001)	0.0402	0.9520	0.9782	0.9785
H_B: $\Lambda_x\Lambda_y\Gamma$	0.9884	0.9893	0.0622	0.0658	134.5373/73 (0.0000)	0.0420	0.9431	0.9729	0.9731
H_C: $\Lambda_x\Lambda_y\Gamma\Theta_\delta\Theta_\varepsilon$	0.9882	0.9892	0.0617	0.0671	136.1659/83 (0.0002)	0.0366	0.9424	0.9766	0.9767
H_D: $\Lambda_x\Lambda_y\Gamma\Theta_\delta\Theta_\varepsilon\Phi\Psi$	0.9879	0.9890	0.0621	0.0674	138.9323/87 (0.0003)	0.0353	0.9412	0.9772	0.9772

Table 8.3 Chi-Square Difference Tests of Overall Fit by Hypothesis

Test	χ^2 Difference	df Difference	p-value
$H_B - H_A$	20.9973	9	0.0126
$H_C - H_B$	1.6286	10	0.9984
$H_C - H_A$	22.6259	19	0.2542
$H_D - H_C$	2.7664	4	0.5976
$H_D - H_B$	4.3950	14	0.9925
$H_D - H_A$	25.3923	23	0.3303

discussed below provide some additional context supporting this contention, but additional research retesting these hypotheses on different data would help clarify the ambiguity between Chi-square results and other tests of model fit.

Hypothesis C

Hypothesis C coupled the constraints in the first two hypotheses with an additional constraint of invariant measurement error variances. The results of this test suggest that measurement error variances do not vary by wave. The GFI for each model exceeded 0.98 and the standardized RMR was less than 0.07. The Chi-square was statistically significant (p=0.0002), but the RMSEA (0.0366), NFI (0.9424), CFI (0.9766), and IFI (0.9767) indicate that, overall, imposing these constraints across the waves did not result in a poor model fit. The statistically insignificant Chi-square difference test (p=0.9984) comparing Hypothesis C to Hypothesis B illustrates that adding the constraint of invariant measurement error does not appreciably further reduce the fit of the model. Similarly, the statistically insignificant Chi-square difference test (p=0.2542) comparing Hypothesis C to Hypothesis A illustrates adding the restrictions implied in Hypothesis C does not statistically reduce the overall fit of the model, providing additional evidence that the factor loadings may be invariant, contrary to the results comparing Hypothesis B to Hypothesis A.

Hypothesis D

Hypothesis D further constrains the model to require the covariance of the latent constructs to be invariant. The group and global assessment statistics of this model were virtually identical to those in Hypothesis C. That is, all measures indicated that the covariance of the latent constructs were invariant except the strict Chi-square (p=0.0003). The Chi-square difference test (p=0.5976) also suggested that adding this constraint did not significantly reduce the fit of the model. Furthermore, the Chi-square difference tests suggest that the more restrictive model in Hypothesis D fits the data just as well as the less restrictive models tested in Hypotheses B (p=0.9925), and A (p=0.3303). Of particular importance is the contrast of Hypothesis D to A. This shows the more restrictive model, which includes invariant dimensions and patterns, factor loadings, measurement error, and latent construct covariances fits the data just as well as the least restrictive model that simply implies invariant dimensions and patterns across the two sets of data. This tends to undermine the results of the contrast of Hypothesis B to A, providing additional evidence that the factor loadings are likely invariant.

Factor Scores

Latent constructs have no scale of their own. To estimate them they must be given a scale (e.g., by constraining a factor loading to one). This process permits the estimation of predicted factor scores to represent latent constructs that are used in the COP measurement model and the path analyses. To interpret the constructs represented by factor scores it is necessary to examine the range of the predicted factor scores for each variable. The specific scale is less important than knowing the scale. That is, it makes little difference whether the scale ranges −100 to 100 or from 10 to 20. Both ranges represent an interval scale. Rather, it is more important to know the range of values for the predicted factor scores so that the relative influence of a given change can be interpreted.

Now that the measurement model has been confirmed, it is possible to estimate the factor scores associated with the COP latent constructs and derive their descriptive statistics. The possible values of the factor score, determined from when all COP activities are reported at their minimum and maximum values, is 0 to 3.187. In 1997, the derived COP implementation scores ranged from 0.15 to 2.96, with a mean of 1.82 and a standard deviation of 0.62. In 1999, the derived COP implementation scores ranged from 0.41 to 3.13, with a mean of 2.03 and a standard deviation of 0.62. On average, COP implementation increased 0.21 units over this two-year period. Given the emphasis on the community policing philosophy during this time period, it is somewhat surprising the increase was not higher.

This information will be particularly useful to facilitate the interpretation of the path analyses. Again, the importance of these numbers is in the intervals they represent; for both years, I discuss how variables can affect derived units of COP implementation, a measure shown here to have a range of just over 3 units. Appendix B summarizes the process by which others can calculate estimates of COP implementation based on this model, and Appendix C offers the estimates of COP implementation for each sample police organization calculated for this study.

Structural Model of Community Policing Implementation

Determinants of Community Policing Implementation

Having examined the validity of the COP implementation model and its variables both within and across years, I turn to what explains its variation. The model of Figure 7.3 on page 70 suggests the extent of COP implementation in 1999 was a function of eleven exogenous organizational context variables (e.g., organization size and task scope, jurisdiction demographic characteristics), four exogenous variables accounting for structural complexity in 1997 (e.g., stations, occupational differentiation), three exogenous variables associated with structural control in 1997 (e.g., centralization, administrative weight), and the level of COP implementation in 1997. The model accounted for 28 percent of the variation in COP implementation. This is similar to other models explaining COP implementation. I discuss the relationships of each group of variables below.

Organizational Context

Table 8.4 displays the effects of the organizational context variables on COP implementation. I discuss each of these eleven variables below.

Organization Size. The full model shows organization size does not affect COP implementation. Recall that Maguire et al. (1998) suggested the influence of organization size on COP adoption may be bidirectional, with larger agencies having greater resources but smaller agencies facing greater demands for COP. I hypothesized that after controlling for COP funding per employee, which captures much but not all the cost of implementing COP, size would still positively influence the implementation of COP. The analysis did not confirm this hypothesis. This result is not consistent with the work of Maguire et al. and Zhao (1996), who found a positive association between organization size and COP implementation. One possible reason for the discrepancy is the focus of Maguire et al. on "nonurban" police agencies and my focus on "larger" agencies. My result is consistent with

Table 8.4 Test of Impact of the Organizational Context on COP Implementation and Organizational Structure

	1999 COP	1999 Organizational Structure			
1990–1997	COP Implementation	Stations	Occupational Differentiation	Formalization	Administrative Weight
Organizational Context					
Organization Size (LN)	.0652/.0924[b]	-.3358/-.0171	.0000/-.0005	-.1337/-.0891	.5570/.0646
St. Error	.0540	.7236	.0043	.1252	.6342
z-ratio	1.2090	-.4640	-.0114	-1.0674	.8783
Organization Age	.0032/.1709**	-.0009/-.0017	.0001/.0348	.0014/.0355	.0081/.0350
St. Error	.0010	.0159	.0001	.0023	.0120
z-ratio	3.2014	-.0559	.8184	.6075	.6755
Task Scope	.0049/.0125	-.0396/-.0036	.0050/.0874*	.1022/.1224*	-.1981/-.0412
St. Error	.0181	.2892	.0021	.0421	.2147
z-ratio	.2716	-.1370	2.3801	2.4296	-.9227
Race Heterogeneity	.1793/.0462	1.6172/.0150	.0149/.0266	.4561/.0564	-2.4817/-.0524
St. Error	.2114	3.3902	.0243	.4917	2.5040
z-ratio	.8483	.4770	.6132	.9459	-.9911
Income Heterogeneity	1.4790/.0264	21.6008/.0139	-.3201/-.0395	4.2492/.0357	-4.2740/-.0062
St. Error	2.9408	47.3165	.3381	6.8252	34.8761
z-ratio	.5029	.4565	-.9467	.6226	-.1225
Unemployment	-.0206/-.0903	-.1539/-.0242	-.0044/-.1339**	-.0014/-.0030	-.0237/-.0085
St. Error	.0123	.1958	.0014	.0285	.1444
z-ratio	-1.6830	-.7857	-3.1469	-.0507	-.1639
Chief Turnover	-.0840/-.1237**	.4320/.0229	-.0038/-.0388	-.1241/-.0861	-.5215/-.0629
St. Error	.0317	.4977	.0036	.0732	.3768
z-ratio	-2.6448	.8681	-1.0721	-1.6970	-1.3842

(Continued)

Table 8.4 (Continued)

1990-1997	1999 COP		1999 Organizational Structure		
Organizational Context	COP Implementation	Stations	Occupational Differentiation	Formalization	Administrative Weight
Population Mobility	.0097/.1313*	.0096/.0047	-.0005/-.0459	-.0044/-.0279	-.0507/-.0560
St. Error	.0043	.0664	.0005	.0099	.0503
z-ratio	2.2581	.1442	-1.0400	-.4452	-1.0066
Env. Capacity	.0061/.0083	.5403/.0265	-.0005/-.0044	-.0877/-.0563	-.3634/-.0406
St. Error	.0338	.5385	.0039	.0780	.3988
z-ratio	.1793	1.0033	-.1208	-1.2141	-.9111
Funding Incentive[a]	.0167/.0994*	-.0812/-.0174	-.0002/-.0092	.0236/.0662	-.0150/-.0073
St. Error	.0074	.1194	.0009	.0173	.0882
z-ratio	2.2493	-.6800	-.2600	1.3666	-.1703
Western Region	.1540/.2493***	-.5743/-.0335	.0229/.2567***	.3779/.2881***	1.6492/.2187***
St. Error	.0437	.6009	.0045	.1009	.5055
z-ratio	3.5224	-.9556	5.1327	3.7432	3.2623
R-square	**.3343**	**.7739**	**.5725**	**.2002**	**.3702**

* $p<.05$, ** $p<.01$, *** $p<.001$

[a] COP funds per full-time equivalent employee is measured in thousands of dollars.

[b] The cells corresponding to the intersection of each exogenous and endogenous variable represent the estimated unstandardized and standardized coefficients, respectively. These results are based upon full estimation of the 5-equation system.

King's (1998) study of large municipal agencies that also failed to find a relationship between organization size and COP implementation. It appears that organization size does not affect COP implementation in large, municipal agencies.

Organization Age. My analysis shows age (z-ratio of 3.20) to be a significant influence of COP implementation. On average, COP implementation is 0.0032 units greater for each additional year of age, or 0.032 for each additional ten years of age. This is inconsistent with King's (1998) finding that age was unrelated to whether a police organization implemented COP and had regular assignment of community officers. Yet, this finding does offer some support for King's finding that organization age is positively associated with COP programmatic innovation (e.g., community crime prevention programs and foot patrol). This suggests organizations with greater historical experience are more likely to find value in and be better able to implement COP.

Task Scope. The analysis failed to show any influence of task scope on COP implementation. Competing perspectives suggested that task variability might make police organizations more likely to implement COP as a means to provide holistic services or less likely to implement COP so as to seal the organizations from various demands. This analysis provides no support for either perspective, although it also cannot answer the question of whether task scope simply has no effect rather than competing effects that offset each other. Further research should seek to isolate these competing effects to fully explore the nature of their impact, if any.

Race and Income Heterogeneity, Unemployment, Chief Turnover, and Population Mobility. Controlling for other influences, two of these five community characteristics appear to have affected COP implementation. Police chief turnover (z-ratio of −2.2581) negatively affected COP implementation; for each additional chief an organization had, COP implementation fell by 0.0840 units on my scale with a range of nearly three units. Population mobility (z-ratio of 2.2581) positively influenced COP implementation. The estimate of this relationship suggests that for a single percent increase in population mobility, COP implementation increases 0.0097 units. The other community characteristics did not appear to have an influence on COP implementation.

These findings do not illustrate a consistent relationship between community characteristics and COP implementation. Police chief turnover and population mobility each capture some aspect of uncertainty in the environment of police organizations, yet their impact on COP implementation varies. The negative influence of police chief turnover in my model may support Thompson's (1967) claim that organizations in uncertain environments are more likely to seal off their organizations from the external environment and therefore be less likely to support COP implementation. The positive influence of population mobility on COP implementation may support Burns and Stalker's (1961) contention that organizations in uncertain environments are more organic and therefore more likely to implement COP. The inconsistency of these findings suggests that both hypotheses may, to some extent, be correct, and environmental uncertainty may both facilitate and impede COP implementation. Moreover, the analysis indicates that the impetuses of these alternative influences manifest themselves in variables measuring specific aspects of uncertainty. The frequency with which police organizations change leadership is important for determining the extent to which they guard their internal processes and protect their core technologies. Changing leadership may also hamper community policing because those who must implement it may be uncertain as to whether there will be executive commitment to it over time by new chiefs. This is not surprising, given their need to function consistently despite fluidity in leadership. By contrast, those that face uncertainty arising from serving mobile populations may respond by becoming more flexible and adaptable to the needs of the community.

Environmental Capacity. The analysis did not confirm an association between environmental capacity and COP implementation. There are two potential explanations for this. First, it is possible that external entities such as employee associations or unions and civilian review boards have no effect on COP implementation. The second and perhaps more plausible explanation is that such entities have competing, and offsetting, influences on COP implementation. For example, collective bargaining agreements and police unions may be less likely to encourage COP because of the possibility of adverse effects on employees (e.g., eliminating positions), while civilian review and accreditation boards may encourage COP for its emphasis on collaboration between the police and community. Such offsetting effects would explain the lack of statistical association between environmental capacity and COP implementation. Future research should consider distinguishing these effects.

Funding Incentives. COP funding (z-ratio of 2.2493) facilitated COP implementation. Controlling for other variables, the model suggests that every additional $1,000 of COP funding per full-time equivalent employee increased COP implementation by 0.0167 units. This confirms my hypothesis that organizations receiving a greater level of funding for COP implement it to a greater extent than those receiving less funding. On average, each organization received $3,286 per employee; such an increase would increase COP implementation by about 0.07 units. Given that the measure of COP implementation for 1999 ranged from 0.41 to 3.13, this finding suggests it would take a very large increase to effect a sizeable change in COP implementation. For example, an organization of 100 officers would require $328,600 to effect a change of just 0.07 units, and more than $4.5 million to effect a change of 1.00 units on my measure of COP implementation. Although statistically related, funding incentives do not seem to be a prominent predictor of COP implementation, nor a panacea for its implementation.

Region. Having a location in the West (z-ratio of 3.5224) has a positive effect on COP implementation. Police organizations in the West have, on average, implemented 0.1540 units more than organizations elsewhere. This finding supports other studies (e.g., Maguire et al., 1997; Zhao, 1996) that have shown police organizations in the West to be more progressive in their philosophies and practices. This work does not shed light on why regional differences exist. As Maguire et al. (1997) summarize, the regional differences may stem from differences in local political structures (Wilson, 1968), innovation diffusion networks (Weiss, 1992 and 1997), and historical development of the police (Langworthy and Travis, 1994).

Organizational Structure

I differentiate the effects of organizational structure by those resulting from structural complexity (e.g., occupational differentiation) and those resulting from structural control (e.g., centralization, administrative weight). Table 8.5 presents summary statistics for these variables.

Structural Complexity — Stations, Occupational Differentiation, Ranks, and Functional Units. No measure of structural complexity had a statistically significant association with COP implementation. That is, these results indicate that structural complexity does not determine COP implementation. Given the importance of organizational structure to the COP philosophy and in the innovation literature that suggests organic structures enhance innovation, this finding is striking.

Structural Control — Centralization, Formalization, and Administrative Weight. There was no statistically significant effect of centralization or administrative weight on the implementation of COP. Formalization (z-ratio of 2.02) positively influenced COP implementation; for each formal policy directive (of a total of ten) queried in the LEMAS survey, COP implementation increases by 0.0146 units. Though not substantively large, this finding is noteworthy. I had hypothesized that formalization would have a negative influence on COP implementation because it is inconsistent with the philosophy of COP. The findings of my model not only counter this hypothesis, but also the idea that organic organizations are more innovative, though the findings support Duncan's (1976) contention (as well as contentions of Damanpour, 1991, and Wilson, 1966) that mechanistic structures are better able to implement (though not necessarily create) innovations. Given the complexity of COP, it may be that formal procedures help coordinate the efforts that facilitate its implementation.

Community Policing Implementation
As expected, the level of COP implementation in 1997 statistically determined the level of its implementation in 1999 (z-ratio of 4.9600). A one-unit increase in 1997 COP implementation is associated with a 0.2473 unit increase in 1999 COP implementation (See Table 8.5). This suggests that COP implementation is partially sustainable on its own. That is, efforts to implement COP will have lasting, although small and diminishing, effects. What is surprising is that this relationship is not stronger. This suggests that, on average, the extent to which a police organization implements COP is largely unrelated to its past experience in conducting COP activities. This is inconsistent with other aspects of

Table 8.5 Test of Simultaneous Impact between COP Implementation and Organizational Structure

1997 Organizational Structure	1999 COP		1999 Organizational Structure		
	COP Implementation	Stations	Occupational Differentiation	Formalization	Administrative Weight
Stations	-.0033/-.0813[a]	.9855/.8777***	—	.0048/.0560	-.0262/-.0531
St. Error	.0023	.0365	—	.0053	.0271
z-ratio	-1.4379	27.0282	—	.9038	-.9693
Occupat. Diff.	.2357/.0373	—[b]	.5409/.5930***	-.1127/-.0084	10.3487/.1342**
St. Error	.3361		.0359	.7261	3.9897
z-ratio	.7013		15.0722	-.1552	2.5939
Ranks	.0863/.0789	—	—	.4475/.1926**	2.0151/.1508**
St. Error	.0628			.1458	.7429
z-ratio	1.3753			3.0698	2.7125
Functional Units	-.0041/-.0214	—	—	.0176/.0437	.1510/.0650
St. Error	.0097			.0226	.1155
z-ratio	-.4169			.7804	1.3074
Centralization	.0047/.0640	—	—	—	—
St. Error	.0033				
z-ratio	1.4491				
Formalization	.0146/.0904*	—	—	.1228/.3572***	—
St. Error	.0073			.0169	
z-ratio	2.0163			7.2755	
Admin. Weight	.0012/.0146	—	—	—	.4380/.4346***
St. Error	.0042				.0502
z-ratio	.2853				8.7295

(Continued)

Table 8.5 *(Continued)*

1997 COP	1999 COP Implementation	1999 Organizational Structure			
	COP Implementation	Stations	Occupational Differentiation	Formalization	Administrative Weight
COP Implementation	.2473/.2496***	.0766/.0028	-.0107/-.0749	-.0866/-.0412	-.3706/-.0306
St. Error	.0499	.7729	.0055	.1159	.5832
z-ratio	4.9600	.0991	-1.9364	-.7470	-.6355
R-square	.3343	.7739	.5725	.2002	.3702

* $p < .05$, ** $p < .01$, *** $p < .001$

[a] The cells corresponding to the intersection of each exogenous and endogenous variable represent the estimated unstandardized and standardized coefficients, respectively. These results are based upon full estimation of the 5-equation system.

[b] "____" represents a relationship not specified in the model.

police organizations, such as structure, that typically change very little over time so are highly related to past experience. This finding also raises the issue of potential measurement error. As noted above, it is possible that respondents are not properly characterizing their COP efforts in each wave of the LEMAS survey, thereby indicating the possibility of limited test-retest reliability of the COP measure.

Relative Impacts on Community Policing Implementation
Given the ultimate objective of discovering elements that facilitate and impede COP implementation, it is worth discussing the relative impacts of the elements discussed above. These are depicted by the effects of predictor variables in Tables 8.4 and 8.5 shown standardized for changes in standard deviations in both the predictor variable and COP implementation.

The most influential predictor of a police organization's COP implementation was its previous level of implementation (standardized coefficient of 0.2496). This suggests working to implement COP has a lasting effect on its implementation, but the effect is not as large as one would expect and may be an indication of measurement error.

Among organization context variables, the greatest standardized effects were those of Western location (0.2493), organization age (0.1709), population mobility (0.1313), police chief turnover (-0.1237), and funding incentives (0.0994). It is noteworthy that funding incentives had the smallest relative impact.

Two of these five variables, population mobility and police chief turnover, are community characteristics. As these pertain to uncertainty in the environment of police organizations, this lends some support for the importance of task-related determinants of COP. The importance of organization age is suggestive of this as well. Nevertheless, the model does not provide support for the effects of other task-related determinants such as organization size, task scope, race or income heterogeneity, and unemployment. Two of the three institutional-related determinants were associated with COP implementation. Environmental capacity does not help account for variation in COP implementation, but funding incentives and Western region do. As mentioned earlier, the significance of funding incentives supports resource dependency theory as well. Nonetheless, these findings are illustrative in that they confirm multiple types of demands influence police organizations. These results are consistent with those of Hirsch (1975), Mastrofski (1998), Meyer and Rowan (1997), Meyer and Scott (1983), and Parsons (1961), who proposed that both task and institutional demands are critical for understanding the functioning of (police) organizations.

The analysis deemed none of the structural complexity and only one structural control measure statistically significant, with a single standard deviation increase in formalization enhancing COP implementation by 0.0904 standard deviations. Formalization had the smallest standardized effect of all the statistically significant determinants.

It appears that formalization through policy, which is a mechanistic form of organizational structure, is associated with COP implementation. This suggests that, among organizational structure variables, structural control mechanisms may determine COP implementation, whereas structural complexity mechanisms, such as number of stations and occupational differentiation, do not.

Determinants of Structural Complexity

Stations and occupational differentiation were the two endogenous variables pertaining to structural complexity. The model predicted that each of these variables would be influenced by the same eleven organizational context variables shown in Figure 7.3 on page 70 and Table 8.4 on page 83. The model also accounted for previous levels of structural complexity in terms of stations and occupational differentiation and COP implementation in 1997. In all, the variables explained 77 percent of the variation in stations and 57 percent of the variation in occupational differentiation. Given the purpose of discovering factors that affect organizational structure, I discuss the effects of each contextual variable on the two structural complexity measures.

Organizational Context

Table 8.4 on page 83 summarizes the results pertaining to the impact of organizational context on structural complexity.

Organization Size. Organization size had no statistically significant influence on either of the structural complexity measures. That is, overall, organization size appears to have no impact on structural complexity. This finding counters Blau's (1970) theory of differentiation as well as the findings of Maguire (2003) and King (1998) on police organization size and structure. Recall that Langworthy (1996) found an inverse relationship between organization size and occupational differentiation, suggesting a possible age effect. The work in this book demonstrates that, when controlling for age, organization size has no association with occupational differentiation.

Organization Age. Organization age does not influence either measure of structural complexity; controlling for other variables, older organizations have no more stations or occupational differentiation than younger ones.

Task Scope. Task scope had a statistically significant (z-ratio of 2.3801) positive effect on occupational differentiation, but no effect on the number of stations. Each additional task among the seventeen queried in the LEMAS survey increased occupational differentiation by 0.0050 units. The two competing perspectives of technology suggest that organizations with greater task scope will become more organic or more complex. These results suggest larger task scopes lead to greater complexity. Consistent with Thompson's (1967) perspective, the responsibility for more tasks enhances occupational differentiation. Both Thompson and Perrow (1967) predict a positive relationship between task scope and spatial differentiation, an effect not observed in the analysis. Given these findings, Perrow's perspective that task variability coincides with organic structures is not supported.

Race and Income Heterogeneity. Race and income heterogeneity represent dimensions of community uncertainty for the police. Burns and Stalker (1967) contend that organizations in uncertain environments are more organic, whereas Thompson (1967) contends that such organizations would be more elaborate to seal off their boundaries. I did not find race and income heterogeneity to be associated with either of the structural complexity measures. Similar to Maguire (2003), this suggests that race and income heterogeneity have no significant relationship with structural complexity. Whether this means neither theory is correct, or both are correct but have offsetting effects, is not clear; other variables discussed below suggest varying interpretations.

Unemployment. Local unemployment inversely affects police organization occupational differentiation (z-ratio of −3.15); a 1 percent increase in unemployment reduces occupational differentiation −0.0044 units. This implies that organizations facing greater environmental uncertainty will become more mechanistic. However, it had no effect on spatial differentiation (i.e., the number of stations).

Police Chief Turnover. Maguire (2003) contends that uncertainty that penetrates organizational boundaries may be the most critical form of uncertainty. Nevertheless, police chief turnover, my model's measure of such uncertainty, was unrelated to stations or occupational differentiation. This result provides support for neither Thompson (1967) nor Burns and Stalker (1961).

Population Mobility. The finding with regard to population mobility also failed to support either Thompson (1967) or Burns and Stalker (1961). It was statistically unrelated to stations and occupational differentiation.

Environmental Capacity. Environmental capacity also does not affect stations or occupational differentiation. That is, entities such as unions or civilian review boards in the institutional environment of police organizations appear unrelated to the number of stations and occupational differentiation.

Funding Incentive. COP funding was statistically unrelated to the number of stations and occupational differentiation. This is remarkable given that many COP grants are earmarked for hiring sworn officers.

Region. Police organizations in the West had greater occupational differentiation (z-ratio of 5.13) but were no different in the number of stations they operated. Occupational differentiation in Western police organizations was 0.0229 units greater than elsewhere. Police organizations in the West are somewhat more likely to have characteristics of structural complexity that correspond to the COP philosophy; that is, they are more apt to have nonsworn employees.

Structural Complexity

Table 8.5 on page 89 shows the number of stations (z-ratio of 27.03) and occupational differentiation (z-ratio of 15.07) in 1997 were strongly associated with the 1999 values of these variables. For each additional station an organization had in 1997, it had 0.9855 additional stations in 1999. For each unit increase in occupational differentiation in 1997, the organization had 0.5409 units of occupational differentiation in 1999.

Community Policing Implementation
Table 8.5 shows the extent of COP implementation in 1997 was not related to either measure of structural complexity in 1999. This suggests there is no simultaneous relationship between COP and structural complexity.

Determinants of Structural Control

Two endogenous variables represented structural control in 1999 — formalization and administrative weight. The model (see Figure 7.3 on page 70) specified that these structural control variables be a function of (1) the organizational context variables that influenced structural complexity, (2) the three structural complexity measures of 1997, (3) the 1997 structural control measures, and (4) the extent of COP implementation in 1997. These variables explained 20 percent of the variation in formalization and 37 percent of the variation in administrative weight. I review below the relationship of each of these four groups of variables with the structural control variables.

Organizational Context
Table 8.4 on page 83 summarizes the data on the relationships between the organization context variables and structural control. I review organizational context variables individually below.

Organization Size. Organization size had no significant influence on formalization or administrative weight. This is contrary to propositions set forth by traditional organizational scholars such as Blau (1970), Blau and Schoenherr (1971), Child (1973a), and Hsu et al. (1983), but reaffirms studies of police organizations that generally find little or no relationship between organization size and structural control. Organization size was related to administrative ratios in Langworthy (1986) and to formalization in King (1999), but Maguire's (2003) more comprehensive work revealed it had no statistical association with any structural control measure. My findings provide additional evidence that police organizations differ from other organizations in the variables that influence organizational design.

Organization Age. The analysis found no impact of organization age on formalization or administrative weight. Like those of King (1999) and Maguire (2003), these findings do not support Downs's (1967) contention that older organizations are generally more formal and have heavier administrative structures. Furthermore, having greater experience with which to make decisions does not make a police organization more likely to adopt certain structural elements related to either complexity or control.

Task Scope. Task scope does not influence administrative weight, but it does influence formalization (z-ratio of 2.43). An additional task in 1997 led to 0.1022 additional policy directives in 1999. These findings partly replicate Maguire's (2003) conclusion that task scope does not affect structural controls of formalization or administration.

Race and Income Heterogeneity. I found neither racial nor income heterogeneity to be associated with either structural control measure. This supports Maguire's (2003) conclusion that environmental complexity does not affect structural control.

Unemployment. Unemployment was unrelated to both structural control measures. This finding contradicts Burns and Stalker's (1961) contention that organizations in less uncertain environments exhibit a more mechanical structural form as well as Thompson's (1967) contention that organizations will seek to seal themselves off when threatened by the uncertainty that unemployment represents.

Police Chief Turnover. I did not find a relationship between police chief turnover and the structural control variables. That is, I found no evidence for a relationship between environmental uncertainty and structural control. This supports Maguire's (2003) finding that turnover was unrelated to formalization and administrative weight.

Population Mobility. Population mobility was also unrelated to formalization and administrative weight. This contradicts findings of Thompson (1967) and Burns and Stalker (1961), but is consistent with Langworthy's (1986) finding.

Environmental Capacity. The analysis did not find environmental capacity to affect formalization or administrative weight. This supports Maguire's (2003) finding that environmental capacity is unrelated to structural control. This implies that bodies such as unions or civilian review boards do not lead police organizations to implement more policy directives or change their administrative apparatus.

Funding Incentive. Funding incentives did not alter formalization or administrative weight, and hence can be said to have no effect on structural control. Combined with the lack of a relationship between COP funding and structural complexity, it appears that funding incentives do not represent a major determinant of organizational structure in general.

Region. Region was the only organizational context variable to affect both formalization and administrative weight. Controlling for other variables, the analysis shows Western police organizations have 0.3779 (z-ratio of 3.7432) more policies and 1.6492 percent (z-ratio of 3.2623) greater administrative weight than those elsewhere in the United States. These results were not expected. More policy directives indicate more control typical of less organic organizations.

Structural Complexity

Table 8.5 on page 89 depicts data on the statistical relationship between structural complexity and control. I review the effects of each structural complexity variable below.

Stations. The number of stations a police organization has is not related to its formalization or administrative weight. These findings confirm those of Maguire (2003). Spatial differentiation, while making the structure more complex, does not seem to require police organizations to develop more elaborate structural control mechanisms.

Occupational Differentiation. Occupational differentiation was unrelated to formalization but is related to administrative weight (z-ratio of 2.59). Holding other variables constant, a one-unit increase in occupational differentiation increases administrative weight 10.3487 percent. This evidence, showing police organizations with greater occupational differentiation in 1997 have greater administrative weight in 1999, offers some support for the differentiation-coordination hypothesis that complexity increases the need for coordination (Rushing, 1967).

Ranks. The number of ranks was positively associated with both formalization (z-ratio of 3.0698) and administrative weight (z-ratio of 2.7125). Each additional rank leads to written policy directives in

0.4475 more areas and a 2.0151 percent increase in administrative weight. This also suggests an association between structural complexity and control in large police organizations.

Functional Units. The number of functional units was unassociated with formalization or administrative weight. This does not support the application of the differentiation-coordination hypothesis (Rushing, 1967) to police organizations.

Differentiation-Coordination. The overall findings provide some support for the differentiation-coordination hypothesis, but the relationship is not evident between every measure. Two measures of structural complexity, stations and functional units, were unrelated to either measure of structural control, but occupational differentiation predicted administrative weight and ranks predicted both formalization and administrative weight. In short, there is some evidence suggesting that occupational and hierarchical differentiation elements of structural complexity determine structural control mechanisms in large police organizations, but structural control is not a function of spatial or functional differentiation.

Structural Control

Formalization (z-ratio of 7.2755) in 1997 was associated with the same variable in 1999 and administrative weight (z-ratio of 8.7295) in 1997 was associated with the same variable in 1999. Each additional policy directive in 1997 led to 0.1228 additional directives in 1999; each percentage increase in administrative weight led to a 0.4380 percent increase in 1999.

Community Policing Implementation

Consistent with its lack of effect on structural complexity, COP implementation in 1997 was unrelated to structural control in 1999. This refutes the notion of a simultaneous or mutually reinforcing relationship between COP implementation and structural control.

Model Fit

Overall, the full five-equation model fit the data rather well. Although the strict Chi-square test was statistically significant ($p=0.01$), indicating the model did not fit the data perfectly, the remaining fit measures suggested a good fit. Both the RMSEA (0.07) and Standardized RMR (0.01) were relatively low. Similarly, the fit indices were quite high, with the CFI and IFI at 0.99, the NNFI at 0.95, and the AGFI at 0.89.

Despite the complexity of this model, the fit is fairly good. This is important, given that I created the model in part to overcome the limited scope of previous research in the areas addressed by the model, and there are few if any benchmark models on the subject. Accounting for the contextual and structural elements for explaining organizational structure and COP implementation resulted in a good-fitting model. This conclusion lends additional support for the utility of integrating the complexity of all these relationships into a single model. However, some caution is warranted. As discussed above, a good-fitting model does not necessarily mean it is a true representation of reality (MacCallum, et al., 1993). The model also illustrated that many relationships did not exist. The complexity and comprehensiveness of this model limits the statistical power to detect relationships more than a simpler or more parsimonious model. It would be illustrative to retest this model on a larger sample of police organizations to determine if the existence of greater power substantiates some additional relationships. This may include smaller or county agencies to see if the findings generalize to these types of agencies as well.

The next chapter summarizes the key conclusions reached from analysis of the models.

9

CONCLUSIONS AND
POLICY IMPLICATIONS

Determinants of Community Policing and Its
Relationship with Organizational Structure

The research in this book seeks to identify determinants of COP implementation and delineate its relationship with organizational structure. To accomplish this, I drew on the literatures of policing, organizational theory, innovation, and implementation to develop and test a complex model of COP implementation. This model accounted for the influence of organizational context and structure on COP implementation as well as the impact of COP implementation on organizational structure. The contributions of this analysis include identifying determinants of COP implementation, analysis of the individual and relative impacts of these determinants, improving measurement and analysis of these variables, testing of a simultaneous or mutually reinforcing relationship between organizational structure and COP implementation, reconciling organizational theories, and enhancing implementation research in general. The model also has several limitations, such as the reliance on reported data, limited ability to assess the dosage of measures, a restricted pool of items to estimate community policing, and limited sample size for the complexity of the model.

I found the most influential factor in a police organization's implementation of community policing is its previous level of implementation. This suggests that while initial implementation may be difficult, the efforts are somewhat sustainable over time. Working to implement community policing has lasting effects such that, holding other factors constant, a greater level of community policing implementation at one point in time facilitates future implementation. The impact is fairly small, however, so the effect diminishes quickly over a short period of time. This suggests, unlike other aspects of police organizations (e.g., organizational structure), past experience with COP activities does not necessarily mean a police organization will conduct them in the future. It also raises the question whether respondents correctly and consistently describe their COP activities. The small relationship exhibited here could be a function of measurement error that diminishes test-retest reliability. Future research should explore this relationship and possibility in greater detail.

The importance of organizational context was demonstrated in the relevance of funding incentives, geographic region, population mobility, police chief turnover, and organization age in explaining COP implementation. One of the most striking findings of this study is that although increased COP funding enhances COP implementation, the amount of COP funding per employee had the smallest influence among those variables with a significant effect. This suggests funding incentives are an important but not prominent determinant; money itself is not the key to COP implementation.

Less surprising is the finding that Western police organizations implemented COP more than police organizations elsewhere. This reinforced the findings of other studies (e.g., Maguire et al., 1997; Zhao, 1996). Maguire et al. (1997) contend that such variation is likely due to differences in political structures, innovation diffusion networks, and historical development. Unfortunately, this study does not delineate what makes implementation vary by region. This would be a worthy endeavor.

I found the openness of the organization to the community is a function of uncertainty within the organizational context. The effect of uncertainty, however, depends on its source. Population mobility facilitates COP implementation. This is consistent with Burns and Stalker's (1961) contention that organizations in uncertain environments become more open and adaptive to the environment. Yet, uncertainty resulting from leadership transition, which generally signifies a change in organizational focus and priorities, hinders COP implementation. This is consistent with Thompson's (1967) claim that organizations in uncertain environments will seal themselves off from the environment. To be sure, there are also many practical difficulties of implementing COP under such circumstances.

I found older police organizations implement COP to a greater extent than younger ones. This suggests historical experience facilitates the likelihood of finding utility in and being able to implement COP. Older police organizations may have greater experience in past models of police–community interactions, and may therefore be better able to draw on and be more open to such collaboration.

Organizational structure affected COP implementation through formalization (i.e., the number of policy areas in which an organization has written directives). The size of the impact was rather small, suggesting that if organizational structure is related to COP implementation, it is because mechanistic-type structures coincide with it. This is a noteworthy finding given that organizational studies (e.g., Daft, 1982) often credit organizational innovation to organic rather than mechanistic structures, and the COP philosophy is based on organic ideals.

The link between mechanistic structures and COP implementation may be explained by Duncan's (1976) findings that organizational innovation is divided into stages of initiation and implementation, with formalization (and centralization) impeding the initiation of innovation by reducing the likelihood that new information will be considered within an organization, but facilitating the implementation of innovation by providing singleness of purpose, reducing conflict and ambiguity, and helping the organization gain influence over participants. Damanpour (1991), Zhao (1996), and King (1998) have all illustrated a positive relationship between at least one mechanistic structural element and innovation, including COP. While mechanistic structures may be antithetical to the COP philosophy, they appear to help overcome the difficulty of implementing it. Nevertheless, the relationship between mechanistic characteristics and COP implementation is not likely to be linear. That is, there is likely a point at which increases in formalization cease to enhance COP implementation because it counters the intent and philosophy of COP.

Though there is some link between formalization and COP implementation, there is no overall relationship between organizational structure and COP implementation. This means the two are largely independent of each other, and that there is no simultaneous or mutually reinforcing relationship between them.

Certain police organization structures are no more likely to lead to COP implementation than others, and implementing COP will not lead a police organization to change its structure. Although the literature suggested several elements of organizational context and structure that might be linked to COP implementation, this research indicates the roles of these components manifest themselves only in a few select variables.

Relationships among Community Policing Determinants and Indirect Effects on Community Policing

Most studies of COP implementation examine the total effect of various factors by estimating a single equation. Implicit in such analysis is the assumption that other variables do not mediate the effect of the determinants — that is, variables influencing COP implementation do so only directly and not indirectly. Total effects, however, comprise both direct and indirect effects. The five-equation analysis conducted here clearly established which elements of the organizational context and structure directly influence COP implementation. The analysis also illustrated that determinants have relationships among themselves and that some variables indirectly affect COP implementation through another variable. Specifically, task scope, region, and ranks indirectly affect COP implementation by affecting formalization, a variable that directly affects COP implementation. By revealing the complexity of the relationships among variables affecting COP implementation, I disentangled both the direct and indirect effects so that the intricacies of explaining COP implementation can be better understood. Without such disentanglement, the effects of ranks and task scope on COP implementation, which have no direct effect on it, might not have been discerned.

Analysis of the interrelationships provides very useful information to help inform common conceptions. The organizational context appears to account for some variation in organizational structure, suggesting the structure of police organizations is a response to their organizational context. Task scope, unemployment, and region affect occupational differentiation, task scope and region affect formalization, and region affects administrative weight. At the same time, structural elements, with the exception of formalization, did not influence COP implementation. The lesson derived from exploring these interrelationships is that altering organizational structure to enhance COP will not only have little consequence on implementation, but may also render the organization less able to interact with its organizational context.

Delineating the relationships among the determinants also permitted the testing of the relationship between structural complexity and control. This research ascertained that more structurally complex police organizations tend to have greater structural control mechanisms. Occupational differentiation increased administrative weight and hierarchical differentiation led to greater formalization and administrative weight. Neither spatial nor functional differentiation, though, affected structural control.

Through the exploration of the relationships among the determinants and their impact on COP implementation, this research supported the basic conceptual model of Figure 7.1 on page 56 (with the exception of COP on structure). Not only did the organizational context and an element structure affect COP implementation, elements in each of these components were related to each other. Furthermore, this study showed how nearly all elements in organizational context and structure are relevant for explaining variation in COP implementation and organizational structure. Changes in any of these components must be considered within the context of its relationship to other components and COP implementation.

Measurement of Community Policing Implementation

The measurement model of this research appears to be a reasonable gauge of COP implementation, thereby having practical, academic, and statistical implications.

Practically, the model indicates training police employees in COP principles, developing a formal COP plan, fixing assignments geographically, engaging in problem-solving, and interacting with the community are all empirically linked to and dimensions of a central concept, which I claim, but it may not necessarily be COP, though some components are more associated with it than others. Community interaction is most associated with COP, followed by problem-solving activities and providing COP training to police employees. Less related but still significant elements are a written COP plan and assigning patrol officers and detectives geographically. Training of recruits, and sworn and nonsworn employees are all associated with COP. Though training of sworn officers is most important, even training of citizens contributes to COP, being associated with police–community interaction, the variable most associated with COP.

The measure of COP implementation in this research proved valid for two samples of data. This does not mean the model is a definitive gauge of COP implementation. While the indicators represented in it account for some major components of COP, data limitations preclude the ability to examine other potential indicators. Nevertheless, because the model is consistent with multiple sets of data, it may prove to be a better tool than those used in the past. The model uses variables that can be directly measured to estimate a value for the abstract concept of COP implementation. Although the analytical model underlying this measure is technical, its application is straightforward. The model provides weights for the directly measured variables so that the estimate of COP implementation simply involves multiplying the value of each variable by its weight and summing the products. For those interested,

Appendix B provides a simple two-step process for calculating estimates of COP implementation based on this model.

Through this approach, decision-makers and police practitioners can obtain actual estimates of the progress made in implementing COP. For example, an agency could use this measure to compare the change it experiences over time substantively (in comparison to itself) and relatively (in comparison to other agencies). To be clear, the inherent purpose and utility of this approach lies in comparison. It provides a gauge of change in implementation over time and for comparing implementation across agencies. It is less useful to determine if an organization has successfully implemented COP.

Academically, this model appears to provide a good mechanism for examining changes in and comparisons of COP implementation. It can be used to ascertain whether the overall level of COP implementation has changed over time and to compare COP implementation among police organizations at one point in time or longitudinally. With other variables hypothesized to be associated with COP, this measure can be used to explore factors that are likely to facilitate or impede future or continued COP implementation. It can also be used to investigate whether COP implementation affects measures of police effectiveness.

Statistically, this research demonstrates measurement models appear to provide a good means to gauge COP implementation. This is not surprising, given the versatility of these models to represent numerous constructs. The utility of these models is in their measurement of abstract concepts. This is especially important given the difficulty of defining COP implementation. The research in this book suggests that a single latent construct can be derived from COP activities. That is, information on various COP activities can be pooled to form a single measure of COP implementation that accounts for both the type of available data (dichotomous, ordinal, or interval) and measurement error in the variables. Although the terms that should be included in the model and the reliance on reported data may be debated, this research illustrates the use of an alternative measurement method that may help improve implementation studies.

The ability to construct and use a measurement model of COP implementation is critical for COP research. A principal advantage of this approach over others is that it offers an interval level estimate of COP implementation. This is a considerable improvement in the measurement of COP implementation, which traditionally has relied on less sensitive and less precise dichotomous or ordinal measures. Unlike a single variable measure, these models can be assessed in many ways on how well they fit the data.

Because this is one of the first systematic attempts to construct a measurement of COP implementation using a confirmatory rather than an exploratory approach, subsequent research based on it should proceed conservatively. The results of the current study are promising for gauging COP implementation, but they need to be tested further on additional data. As in other studies, various forms of error in measurement (e.g., respondents giving incorrect answers), data collection methods (e.g., reported as opposed to observed activities), and specification (e.g., important variable missing) limit this research. Measurement is a critical but often overlooked aspect of research. Our knowledge of the relationships among constructs is a function of how well we measure them. Exploring alternative ways to improve measures of COP implementation and other constructs can only facilitate such discoveries. More broadly, this research demonstrated the use of modeling to test relationships, and illustrated a way to distinguish direct and indirect effects. This technique may be useful for learning about other criminal justice issues as well.

Reconciling Organizational Theories

Answering the main question of this research led me to address other broader questions regarding organizational theories. In doing so, I illustrated the utility of combining contingency and institutional theories in an integrated open systems framework. Contingency theory described the importance of task-related variables such as organization size and age, task scope, and environmental uncertainty. Institutional theory detailed the role of institutional-related variables such as environmental capacity, funding incentives, and geographic region. These theories are often thought to be incongruent, but I empirically illustrated the applicability of both to police organizations. Elements derived from both affected some form of organizational structure, and many also influenced COP implementation. In other words, both task and institutional determinants were important for understanding the form and function of large, municipal police organizations. This suggests that isolating these theories for use in police studies oversimplifies and misrepresents the actual relationship between the organization and its context. Some variables may also be indicative of other theories (e.g., funding incentives for community policing may be just as related to resource dependency theory). The purpose of this research is to draw on theories to identify determinants as opposed to actually testing theories. The theories are helpful in this regard, but further research seeking to test these theories must examine more closely which variables correspond to specific theories, and relate them to outcomes such as effectiveness or legitimacy.

Implementation Research

The research in this book seeks to address many concerns of implementation research. First, it drew on literatures of policing, organizational theory, innovation, and implementation to highlight the potential determinants of COP implementation and the research among them. Second, the model it developed could perhaps be used in studying implementation of other criminal justice policies, programs, and innovations. For example, task and institutional environments may help explain variation in use of alternative sentences as well as in educational and other programming offered to inmates in correctional facilities. Third, this analysis illustrated how to derive better measures of constructs important for implementation. Fourth, I showed that use of measurement models not only enhances the precision of construct estimates, but also can be used to obtain interval-level estimates of implementation. This allows implementation to be represented on a continuum. Finally, this analysis derived information regarding implementation through the statistical comparison of a large number of organizations. Its findings are therefore more generalizable than those relying on only a single or a few cases.

APPENDIX A

ANALYTICAL PROCESS OF STRUCTURAL EQUATION MODELING

I estimated and assessed latent constructs via confirmatory factor analysis consistent with the procedures described by Bollen (1989). These stages apply to structural models as well and therefore represent the process by which I conducted the structural analysis. The stages of this process include specification, determining the implied covariance matrix of the model, identification, estimation, assessment, and respecification of each model. Appendix B provides a two-step guide for calculating COP implementation based on the results of this process, and Appendix C offers the actual estimates derived from this process.

Specification

Before measurement models can be assessed they must be specified. Indicators are theoretically related to their corresponding constructs and all other relationships (e.g., correlated errors) are prescribed. More formally, this can be represented as

$$x = \Lambda_x \xi + \delta$$

where x represents the directly measured variables, ξ are the latent constructs, Λ_x are the coefficients of the impact of the latent on observed variables, and δ are the errors of measurement. The models as described above have already been specified as I detailed which directly observed variables served as the measures for each of the constructs.

Determine the Implied Covariance Matrix

At the most basic level, the hypothesis of any structural equation model is that

$$\Sigma = \Sigma(\theta)$$

where Σ is the population covariance matrix of the observed variables, and $\Sigma(\theta)$ is the covariance matrix written as a function of the model parameters freely estimated in θ — the vector of model parameters (Bollen, 1989). This suggests that the elements in the covariance matrix, based on actual data, match those specified by the model in the implied covariance matrix. Therefore, the covariance matrix can be written as a function of the model parameters. Identification, estimation, and model assessment are predicated on this fact.

Identification

Identification has to do with whether a unique solution for each of the parameters in the model exists. This is a function of the model and not the data or sample size. Identification is the process of showing that the parameters in $\Sigma(\theta)$ can be known. There are two general types of identification, local and global. Local identification implies that within a close range of θ_1 there is no other set of parameters, θ_2, for which the elements are the same. Global identification implies that for any set of parameters, no other will lead to the same covariance matrix. Global identification implies local identification. Model identification is further divided into levels. Unidentified models, which cannot be estimated, occur when at least one parameter is not known to be identified. An over-identified model is one where all parameters are known to be identified and at least one parameter is over-identified. Over-identification of a parameter occurs when there is more information than necessary to identify it. Finally, just or exactly identified models are those where all parameters are identified without any additional information.

For a measurement model to be identified, a scale must be given to the latent construct. As latent constructs theoretically impact directly measured variables, each of which could be measured differently, they have no scale of their own. I chose to scale the latent construct by constraining a factor loading, or the estimated effect of the latent construct on an observed measure, to one.[1] For each model, I scaled the latent construct to the measured variable that was most theoretically related to the construct. For example, I estimated the COP implementation latent construct from the measures pertaining to COP training, written COP plan, fixed assignment, problem-solving, and citizen interaction. I scaled the construct to problem-solving because the literature clearly establishes it as a means of police–community collaboration (this is depicted in Figure 7.2 with the "1" on the arrow pointing from the COP implementation construct to the problem-solving variable). Once I scaled each latent construct, I used the various rules of identification detailed in Bollen (1989) and Rigdon (1995) to ensure each of the models were globally identified. Except where noted, all the measurement models were over-identified.

Estimation

Maximum likelihood was used to estimate the measurement models. This method of estimation has several desirable properties. Maximum likelihood estimators are asymptotically unbiased, consistent, asymptotically the most efficient among consistent estimators, and asymptotically approximate a normal distribution (Bollen, 1989).

Essentially, maximum likelihood executes an iterative process by which it chooses values of parameters, compares them to the sample covariance matrix, and readjusts the estimates to make them correspond to the sample covariance matrix as much as possible. In other words, it selects parameters that maximize the probability of obtaining the specific sample. More formally, maximum likelihood attempts to estimate

$$S = \Sigma(\Theta)$$

where S is the sample covariance matrix and $S = \Sigma(\Theta)$ represents the structural parameters implied by the model. Maximum likelihood conducts this process by minimizing the fit function

$$F_{ML} = \log|\Sigma(\Theta)| + tr[S\Sigma^{-1}(\Theta)] - \log|S| - q$$

where q is the number of observed variables. A perfect fit occurs when the fit function is zero. The objective, of course, is to minimize the fit function.

To ensure proper estimation of the measurement models, I accounted for the level of the data in the estimation process. As detailed above, the observed variables in the models I seek to test are interval, ordinal, as well as dichotomous. Bollen (1989) discusses the dangerous consequences of treating all variables as if they were continuous. Some of these consequences may include adversely affecting the Chi-square fit statistic and tests of statistical significance, attenuating the standardized coefficient estimates, and causing correlation among the measurement errors. To account for these differences in scale, I calculated in PRELIS the polyserial correlation matrix and asymptotic covariance matrix for every model containing ordinal and dichotomous observed variables. Using LISREL, I then weighted the polyserial correlation matrix by the asymptotic covariance matrix in a weighted least squares estimation of the model. When all the observed variables in a given model were interval level, I simply estimated the model from the covariance matrix of the variables.

Assessment of Fit

There are two types of assessments required to evaluate how well a given model fits the data. The first is the component fit and the second is the overall model fit. The component fit refers to the fit of individual elements within the model. To assess the component fit, I examined the unstandardized and standardized parameter estimates, including their sign and significance, statistical significance of the variance of the latent construct, squared multiple correlations, error variances, and various covariance matrices to ensure first that the results made sense and second that the component fit was good (e.g., no negative error variances or squared multiple correlations, or squared multiple correlations greater than unity).

The model fit represents how well the model as a whole corresponds to the data. I assessed the model fit by comparing the results of several fit measures, all of which essentially attempt to gauge the closeness of to $S = \Sigma(\hat{\theta})$. These included the Chi-square test statistic, Root Mean Square Error of Approximation (RMSEA), Standardized Root Mean Square Residual (RMR), Normed Fit Index (NFI) or Nonnormed Fit Index (NNFI), Incremental Fit Index (IFI), Comparative Fit Index (CFI), and Goodness of Fit Index (GFI) or Adjusted Goodness of Fit Index (AGFI).

The first goodness of fit statistic I utilized to assess model fit was the Chi-square test statistic (Bollen, 1989), which is defined as

$$\chi^2 = (N\text{-}1)F_{\text{ML}}, \; df = .5(q)(q + 1) - t$$

where N is the sample size and t is the number of free parameters in θ. The null hypothesis is that $\Sigma = \Sigma(\theta)$, so it is not desirable to reject the null hypothesis. This is a very stringent test of whether the model fits the data perfectly. As the Chi-square test may be too restrictive, I employed several other fit measures.

The second fit measure I utilized was the Root Mean Square Error of Approximation (RMSEA) as described by Steiger (1990; Steiger & Lind, 1980). This measure is calculated as

$$RMSEA = \sqrt{\frac{(\chi^2 - df)/(N\text{-}1)}{df}}$$

According to Browne and Cudeck (1993), this estimate of discrepancy per degree of freedom indicates a better fit when the value is closest to zero. While conceding that these guidelines are not infallible, they advise that an RMSEA of 0.05 or less suggests a close fit, a value of 0.08 or less indicates a reasonable fit, and a value greater than 0.10 represents a poor-fitting model.

The third model fit measure I employed was the Standardized Root Mean Square Residual (Standardized RMR) as described in Joreskog and Sorbom (1996). The Standardized RMR estimates the average of the fitted residuals and is determined by the formula

$$RMR = \left[2 \sum_{i=1}^{q} \sum_{j=1}^{i} \frac{(s_{ij} - \hat{\sigma}_{ij})^2}{q(q+1)} \right]^{1/2}$$

As an indicator of the size of the fitted residuals, values of this measure that are closest to zero suggest a better fit.

The Nonnormed Fit Index (NNFI) was the fourth measure I used to assess model fit (Tucker and Lewis, 1973). This measure is also referred to as the Tucker-Lewis Index (TLI) and ρ_2. The NNFI is defined as

$$NNFI = \frac{\chi_b^2 / df_b - \chi_m^2 / df_m}{\chi_b^2 / df_b - 1}$$

where χ_b^2 is the Chi-square test statistic of the "baseline model" (i.e., the most restrictive model possible) and χ_m^2 is the Chi-square test statistic of the "maintained model" that is hypothesized. As Bollen (1989) explains, the numerator of this index compares the worst possible fit to the fit of the hypothesized model. This measure defines the best fit as the expected value of χ_m^2/df_m, which equals one since the expected Chi-square value is its degrees of freedom. The denominator then compares the worst fitting model (χ_b^2/df_b) to the best fitting model (1). The best fitting model will result in a NNFI value of one as the numerator and denominator reduce to the same value. Thus, values approaching one indicate better fitting models. The NNFI is used to assess the structural model, whereas Bentler and Bonett's (1980) Normed Fit Index (NFI) is used to assess the measurement model. The NFI, also known as the Bentler-Bonett Index or Δ_1, is calculated as

$$NFI = \frac{\chi_b^2 - \chi_m^2}{\chi_b^2}$$

One difficulty of this measure, unlike the NNFI, is that the index is a function of the number of model parameters. The use of multiple measures of fit helps to account for this deficiency.

Bollen's (1989) Incremental Fit Index, or Δ_2, served as the fifth means to assess model fit. This measure is computed as

$$IFI = \frac{\chi_b^2 - \chi_m^2}{\chi_b^2 - df_m}$$

As evidenced by the definition, this index also compares the specified model to the baseline model. This index improves Bentler and Bonett's (1980) NFI as the mean of the sampling distribution of the IFI should be influenced less by sample size and an adjustment is made for the degrees of freedom consumed by the model. Estimates of this index approaching one suggest better fitting models.

The sixth measure used to evaluate goodness of fit was Bentler's (1990) Comparative Fit Index (CFI). calculated as

$$CFI = \frac{(\chi_b^2 - df_b) - (\chi_m^2 - df_m)}{\chi_b^2 - df_b}$$

Kaplan (2000) contends, "an argument could be made that the null hypothesis is never exactly true and that the distribution of the test statistic can be better approximated by a noncentral Chi-square with non-centrality parameter λ" (p. 108). Using the difference between the Chi-square statistic and its corresponding degrees of freedom as an estimate of the noncentrality parameter, this index estimates and is adjusted so that it lies within a zero to one range. Values closer to one indicate a better fitting model, and, in practice, this index generally yields estimates that are very close to the IFI.

The final instrument I employed to assess model fit was the Adjusted Goodness of Fit Index (AGFI) proposed by Joreskog and Sorbom (1986),[2] which is based upon the Goodness of Fit Index (GFI). These indices are operationalized as

$$GFI_{ML} = 1 - \frac{tr\left[\left(\Sigma(\hat{\Theta})^{-1} S - I\right)^2\right]}{tr\left[\left(\Sigma(\hat{\Theta})^{-1} S\right)^2\right]}$$

$$AGFI_{ML} = 1 - \left[\frac{q(q+1)}{2df}\right][1 - GFI_{ML}]$$

where I is the identity matrix. Bollen (1989) explains, "The GFI_{ML} measures the relative amount of the variances and covariances in S that are predicted by $[\Sigma(\hat{\Theta})]$. The $AGFI_{ML}$ adjusts for the degrees of freedom of a model relative to the number of variables" (p. 276). Given the superiority of the AGFI to the GFI and the fact that it is based upon the GFI, I used the AGFI and not the GFI to assess model fit (with the exception of the measurement model comparison). Values close to one suggest good fitting models.

The difficulty of these various fit indices is that there are no established "cut-offs" for determining whether a value represents a good fitting value. It is agreed that values closest to a threshold (e.g., one) indicate a better fitting model than ones that are further away. For the purposes of this book, I generally considered each index to represent at least a reasonable fitting model if its values were as follows: NFI, NNFI, IFI, CFI, GFI, and AGFI 0.90 or greater; RMSEA and Standardized RMR 0.10 or less; and a nonsignificant Chi-square. These clearly are not rules or formal standards, but simply a guideline used for this research. Such an approach is necessary, especially because there are so few studies that provide fit indices of similar constructs such that standard values or benchmarks could be created. I use all these fit indices as a holistic measure of fit. That is, I evaluate the evidence provided by all fit measures as a whole and do not reject a model simply because a single measure does not fall within these guidelines. The decision to accept a specification rests on whether the weight of the evidence appears to suggest a proper fitting model.

Revised Analytical Process

Anderson and Gerbing (1988) outline the preferred way in which to estimate and assess measurement models as a two-step process. The first step entails estimating and assessing all measurement models simultaneously in one confirmatory factor analysis, and the second step involves simultaneously estimating the revised measurement models with the structural model. They contend that separating the measurement models from the structural model and estimating them all together enhances the ability to empirically test whether the constructs are unidimensional (i.e., one latent construct determines each set of directly observed measures) and ultimately interpretable. This occurs through the estimation and assessment of the covariances among all the constructs, the loadings of the indicators on the various constructs, and the covariances of the measurement error across indicators within and among constructs. Once unidimensionality has been established within the measurement models, estimating both the measurement and structural model should only slightly change the coefficient estimates for the measurement models (Anderson and Gerbing).

Unfortunately, the complexity of the measurement and structural models in this research precluded the ability to simultaneously estimate the measurement and structural models. Consequently, I followed Bollen's (1989) "piecewise model fitting" strategy, whereby the model is broken into theoretically related components for estimation and assessment.[3] However, I was able to estimate the entire second-order COP measurement model. This process empirically and theoretically tested unidimensionality among all the COP constructs together, which is preferable. This measure is superior to summated indices, and provides fit measures for specific components of the model as well as a set of fit measures for the entire measurement model. This information is useful given that little formal modeling has been conducted in these areas.

As I mentioned above, the complexity of the model precluded the simultaneous estimation of the measurement and structural models. Consequently, I estimated factor scores for the COP implementation latent construct from its corresponding measurement model. A factor score is simply a predicted value of the latent construct estimated from a regression of the latent construct on the directly measured variables in the model. I then substituted these factor scores for the latent construct (i.e., as if the constructs were directly observed) in the structural model and executed a path analysis on the structural model. Although the preferred method would be to estimate the measurement and structural models at the same time without the use of factor scores, utilizing factor scores drastically reduces the degrees of freedom required for estimation and improves the power to detect statistically significant relationships.

APPENDIX B

CALCULATING ESTIMATES OF COMMUNITY POLICING IMPLEMENTATION

Below is a simple two-step process to calculate the implementation of community policing for a given police organization. These estimates, developed from analysis of LEMAS surveys of large U.S. municipal police organizations, are subject to several limitations noted in the text. Users of this measure should familiarize themselves with them in relation to the context in which the measure will be applied. Estimates of this scale can range from 0 to 3.187.

Step One: Score Community Policing Activities

Each of the questions below pertains to a COP activity. Check the appropriate response for each question. Follow the instructions to obtain the correct score for each activity.

In the last three years, what proportion of each of the following types of personnel received at least eight hours of community policing training (e.g., problem-solving, SARA, community partnerships, etc.)?

New officer recruits

_____ None (place 0 on activity score line if checked)

_____ Less than half (place 1 on activity score line if checked)

_____ More than half (place 2 on activity score line if checked)

_____ All (place 3 on activity score line if checked)

RECRUIT COP TRAINING activity score _____

In-service sworn personnel

_____ None (place 0 on activity score line if checked)

_____ Less than half (place 1 on activity score line if checked)

_____ More than half (place 2 on activity score line if checked)

_____ All (place 3 on activity score line if checked)

SWORN COP TRAINING activity score _____

Civilian personnel

_____ None (place 0 on activity score line if checked)

_____ Less than half (place 1 on activity score line if checked)

_____ More than half (place 2 on activity score line if checked)

_____ All (place 3 on activity score line if checked)

NONSWORN COP TRAINING activity score _____

Does your agency have a formally written community policing plan?

_____ No (place 0 on activity score line if checked)

_____ Yes (place 1 on activity score line if checked)

WRITTEN COP PLAN activity score _____

In the last twelve-month period, which of the following did your agency do? (Sum the number of checks and place the value on the activity score line.)

_____ Give patrol officers responsibility for specific geographic areas/beats

_____ Assign detectives to cases based on geographic areas/beats

FIXED ASSIGNMENT activity score _____

In the last twelve-month period, which of the following did your agency do? (Sum the number of checks and place the value on the activity score line.)

_____ Actively encourage patrol officers to engage in SARA-type problem-solving projects on their beat

_____ Include collaborative problem-solving projects in the evaluation criteria of patrol officers

_____ Form problem-solving partnerships with community groups, municipal agencies, or others through specialized contracts or written agreements

PROBLEM-SOLVING activity score _____

In the last twelve-month period, did your agency train citizens in community policing (e.g., community mobilization, problem-solving)?

_____ No (place 0 on activity score line if checked)

_____ Yes (place 1 on activity score line if checked)

CITIZEN TRAINING activity score _____

Does your agency maintain an official site (i.e., "Home Page") on the World Wide Web/Internet?

_____ No (place 0 on activity score line if checked)

_____ Yes (place 1 on activity score line if checked)

WEBSITE activity score _____

In the last twelve-month period, which of the following groups did your agency regularly meet with to address crime-related problems? (Sum the number of checks and place the value on the activity score line)

_____ Neighborhood associations
_____ Tenants' associations
_____ Youth service organizations
_____ Advocacy groups
_____ Business groups
_____ Religious groups
_____ School groups
_____ Other

GROUP MEETINGS activity score _____

Can citizens routinely access crime statistics or crime maps through any of the following methods? (Sum the number of checks and place the value on the activity score line.)

_____ In-person
_____ Telephone
_____ Internet/webpage
_____ Public kiosk/terminal
_____ Newsletter
_____ Newspaper
_____ Radio
_____ Television
_____ Other

DATA ACCESSIBILITY activity score _____

Step Two: Calculate Community Policing Estimate

Below is a worksheet to calculate the estimate of COP implementation. First, copy the activity scores you calculated in step one and place them in their corresponding rows in the score column. Next, multiply each score by its corresponding weight[1] and write the result on the corresponding product line. Finally, add the results listed in the product column. This sum is the estimate of COP implementation for the organization

Activity	Score	Weight	Product
Recruit COP Training	_____ ×	0.0519	= _____
Sworn COP Training	_____ ×	0.1427	= _____
Nonsworn COP Training	_____ ×	0.040	= _____
Written COP Plan	_____ ×	0.111	= _____
Fixed Assignment	_____ ×	0.086	= _____
Problem-solving	_____ ×	0.308	= _____
Citizen Training	_____ ×	0.142	= _____
Website	_____ ×	0.057	= _____
Group Meetings	_____ ×	0.075	= _____
Data Accessibility	_____ ×	0.052	= _____

COP Implementation Estimate = Sum of Products   _____

APPENDIX C

ESTIMATES OF COMMUNITY POLICING IMPLEMENTATION FOR SAMPLE POLICE ORGANIZATIONS, 1997 AND 1999 (SCALE 0-3.187)

		COP Implementation	
Police Organization	State	1997	1999
Abilene Police Department	TX	1.62	1.80
Akron Police Department	OH	1.45	1.20
Albany Department of Police	GA	2.22	2.16
Albany Police Department	NY	1.76	2.01
Albuquerque Police Department	NM	2.88	2.77
Alexandria Police Department	LA	1.65	1.63
Alexandria Police Department	VA	1.67	2.56
Allentown Police Department	PA	1.93	0.96
Amarillo Police Department	TX	1.60	2.25
Anaheim Police Department	CA	2.12	2.48
Anchorage Police Department	AK	0.96	2.43
Anderson Police Department	IN	1.02	1.60
Ann Arbor Police Department	MI	2.68	2.58
Annapolis Police Department	MD	0.91	1.93
Arlington Heights Police Department	IL	1.20	2.72
Arlington Police Department	TX	2.80	2.08
Arvada Police Department	CO	2.71	2.37
Asheville Police Department	NC	2.60	2.22
Atlanta Police Department	GA	1.15	1.17
Atlantic City Police Department	NJ	1.19	1.60
Aurora Police Department	CO	2.18	2.27
Aurora Police Department	IL	1.61	2.63
Austin Police Department	TX	2.20	2.75
Bakersfield Police Department	CA	1.87	2.02
Baltimore Police Department	MD	2.17	2.43
Baton Rouge Police Department	LA	2.37	1.96
Battle Creek Police Department	MI	1.44	1.80
Bayonne Police Department	NJ	2.00	1.24
Baytown Police Department	TX	2.60	1.08
Beaumont Police Department	TX	2.58	1.78

Bellevue Police Department	WA	2.20	2.39
Berkeley Police Department	CA	2.66	2.46
Beverly Hills Police Department	CA	1.32	1.49
Billings Police Department	MT	2.43	1.92
Binghamton Police Department	NY	1.38	1.85
Birmingham Police Department	AL	1.24	2.41
Bloomfield Police Department	NJ	0.73	1.57
Boca Raton Police Department	FL	1.47	2.17
Boise Police Department	ID	1.95	1.41
Bossier City Police Department	LA	0.37	2.35
Boston Police Department	MA	1.72	2.90
Boulder Police Department	CO	2.87	2.13
Boynton Beach Police Department	FL	1.10	1.84
Brea Police Department	CA	2.54	2.72
Bridgeport Police Department	CT	1.86	1.29
Bristol Police Department	CT	1.46	1.82
Brockton Police Department	MA	2.02	1.49
Brookline Police Department	MA	2.25	2.34
Brownsville Police Department	TX	0.78	1.42
Buffalo Police Department	NY	1.81	1.30
Burbank Police Department	CA	1.24	1.37
Cambridge Police Department	MA	1.65	2.13
Camden Police Department	NJ	2.16	1.95
Canton City Police Department	OH	0.63	1.10
Cape Coral Florida Police Department	FL	1.31	2.46
Carrollton Police Department	TX	0.93	2.08
Cedar Rapids Police Department	IA	1.23	2.20
Chandler Police Department	AZ	2.62	2.69
Charleston Police Department	SC	1.80	1.32
Charleston Police Department	WV	2.49	2.66
Charlotte Police Department	NC	2.61	2.40
Chattanooga Police Department	TN	1.63	2.94

(*Continued*)

Table   (*Continued*)

Cheektowaga Police Department	NY	1.67	2.36
Cherry Hill Police Department	NJ	1.18	0.64
Chesapeake Police Department	VA	2.14	2.48
Chicago Police Department	IL	2.49	1.71
Chicopee Police Department	MA	2.05	1.37
Chula Vista Police Department	CA	1.67	2.28
Cincinnati Police Division	OH	1.75	2.54
Clarksville Police Department	TN	1.30	1.21
Clearwater Police Department	FL	1.43	0.79
Cleveland Police Department	OH	1.33	1.79
Clifton Police Department	NJ	0.68	1.11
Colorado Springs Police Department	CO	2.15	1.97
Columbia Police Department	MO	1.34	2.43
Columbia Police Department	SC	2.69	2.03
Columbus Division of Police	OH	1.07	2.36
Columbus Police Department	GA	1.52	1.11
Compton Police Department	CA	1.23	1.46
Concord Police Department	CA	1.56	2.93
Coral Gables Police Department	FL	1.12	0.87
Coral Springs Police Department	FL	2.32	1.01
Corona Police Department	CA	1.24	2.83
Corpus Christi Police Department	TX	1.21	1.57
Costa Mesa Police Department	CA	1.46	2.21
Cranston Police Department	RI	0.30	0.70
Culver City Police Department	CA	1.37	1.54
Dallas Police Department	TX	1.96	2.66
Daly City Police Department	CA	1.83	1.80
Danbury Police Department	CT	1.25	1.95
Davenport Police Department	IA	0.72	0.98
Davies Police Department	FL	0.96	1.78
Dayton Police Department	OH	1.00	2.70
Daytona Beach Police Department	FL	1.73	1.09

Dearborn Police Department	MI	2.55	1.87
Decatur Police Department	IL	2.75	2.62
Delray Beach Police Department	FL	2.18	2.24
Denton Police Department	TX	2.14	2.54
Denver Police Department	CO	1.00	2.40
Des Moines Police Department	IA	2.27	2.99
Detroit Police Department	MI	0.71	1.63
Dothan Police Department	AL	2.04	2.72
Downey Police Department	CA	0.28	1.25
Duluth Police Department	MN	1.78	1.35
Durham Police Department	NC	1.40	1.71
East Chicago Police Department	IN	1.61	1.31
East Hartford Police Department	CT	2.18	1.43
East Orange Police Department	NJ	2.20	2.67
Edison Police Department	NJ	2.01	1.00
El Cajon Police Department	CA	2.11	2.45
El Monte Police Department	CA	2.58	2.02
El Paso Police Department	TX	2.62	2.28
Elgin Police Department	IL	2.23	2.31
Elizabeth Police Department	NJ	1.78	1.46
Erie Bureau of Police	PA	2.13	1.27
Escondido Police Department	CA	2.24	1.68
Eugene Department of Public Safety	OR	1.88	3.08
Evanston Police Department	IL	2.44	2.89
Evansville Police Department	IN	2.17	2.30
Everett Police Department	WA	1.73	1.78
Fayetteville Police Department	NC	2.56	2.47
Flint Police Department	MI	2.46	2.07
Fontana Police Department	CA	1.83	2.44
Fort Collins Police Services	CO	2.82	1.67
Fort Lauderdale Police Department	FL	1.63	1.75
Fort Myers Police Department	FL	1.54	2.27

(*Continued*)

Table   (*Continued*)

Fort Pierce Police Department	FL	1.07	2.59
Fort Smith Police Department	AR	2.16	1.91
Fort Wayne Police Department	IN	2.26	2.94
Fort Worth Police Department	TX	1.72	1.59
Framingham Police Department	MA	2.09	2.70
Fremont Police Department	CA	2.48	3.00
Fresno Police Department	CA	2.24	2.31
Fullerton Police Department	CA	2.67	2.14
Gadsden Police Department	AL	2.39	2.41
Gainesville Police Department	FL	1.95	2.29
Garden Grove Police Department	CA	2.54	2.12
Garland Police Department	TX	2.71	2.10
Gary Police Department	IN	2.31	2.23
Gastonia Police Department	NC	1.42	1.55
Glendale Police Department	AZ	2.69	2.33
Glendale Police Department	CA	2.28	3.03
Grand Prairie Police Department	TX	1.90	2.56
Grand Rapids Police Department	MI	1.52	2.21
Green Bay Police Department	WI	2.17	2.22
Greensboro Police Department	NC	2.09	2.51
Greenville Police Department	NC	0.64	1.55
Greenville Police Department	SC	1.79	2.26
Greenwich Police Department	CT	1.55	1.33
Hamilton Police Department	OH	2.47	1.68
Hammond Police Department	IN	1.43	1.11
Hampton Police Department	VA	1.84	2.35
Harrisburg Bureau of Police	PA	1.31	2.32
Hartford Police Department	CT	2.07	1.48
Hayward Police Department	CA	2.80	2.58
Hempstead Police Department	NY	1.51	2.07
Hialeah Police Department	FL	0.41	0.59
High Point Police Department	NC	1.41	2.84

Hoboken Police Department	NJ	1.88	1.53
Hollywood Police Department	FL	1.90	2.77
Holyoke Police Department	MA	1.78	1.86
Houston Police Department	TX	1.26	1.92
Huntington Beach Police Dept.	CA	2.52	2.61
Huntington Police Department	WV	1.44	1.30
Huntsville Police Department	AL	1.95	2.96
Independence Police Department	MO	2.84	2.51
Indianapolis Police Department	IN	1.98	1.42
Inglewood Police Department	CA	1.67	1.54
Irvine Police Department	CA	2.53	2.28
Irving Police Department	TX	1.77	1.71
Irvington Police Department	NJ	0.84	2.56
Jackson Police Department	MS	1.28	2.23
Jackson Police Department	TN	0.43	2.32
Jacksonville Sheriff's Office	FL	2.39	2.50
Jersey City Police Department	NJ	0.94	1.60
Johnson City Department of Public Safety	TN	2.03	2.63
Joliet Police Department	IL	2.11	2.75
Kalamazoo DPS	MI	1.75	2.34
Kansas City Police Department	MO	1.38	2.95
Kansas City, Kansas Police Department	KS	1.39	1.09
Kenner Police Department	LA	1.40	2.09
Kenosha Police Department	WI	0.77	1.37
Killeen Police Department	TX	1.77	2.35
Knoxville Police Department	TN	2.74	2.45
Kokomo Police Department	IN	2.02	2.65
Lake Charles Police Department	LA	1.92	1.04
Lakeland Police Department	FL	1.39	1.60
Lakewood Police Department	CO	2.69	2.60
Lancaster Bureau of Police	PA	1.65	2.51
Lansing Police Department	MI	1.99	2.28

(*Continued*)

Table (*Continued*)

Laredo Police Department	TX	1.40	1.52
Largo Police Department	FL	1.89	3.03
Las Cruces Police Department	NM	2.16	2.32
Lawrence Police Department	KS	0.92	1.30
Lawrence Police Department	MA	2.19	1.70
Lawton Police Department	OK	0.61	1.06
Lincoln Police Department	NB	2.96	3.05
Linden Police Department	NJ	2.03	1.24
Little Rock Police Department	AR	2.22	2.30
Livonia Police Department	MI	0.35	0.68
Long Beach Police Department	CA	2.32	2.01
Longview Police Department	TX	1.81	1.45
Los Angeles Police Department	CA	2.77	2.86
Louisville Division of Police	KY	1.58	2.58
Lowell Police Department	MA	1.62	2.69
Lubbock Police Department	TX	0.87	2.32
Lynchburg Police Department	VA	2.41	2.22
Lynn Police Department	MA	0.15	2.50
Macon Police Department	GA	1.66	1.58
Madison Police Department	WI	2.30	2.24
Malden Police Department	MA	0.84	2.09
Manchester Police Department	NH	1.83	2.60
Marietta Police Department	GA	0.68	2.39
McAllen Police Department	TX	1.61	2.22
Melbourne Police Department	FL	2.38	3.04
Memphis Police Department	TN	2.32	1.48
Meriden Police Department	CT	1.90	1.66
Mesa Police Department	AZ	2.36	2.84
Mesquite Police Department	TX	1.37	0.81
Metropolitan Nashville Police Department	TN	1.82	1.90
Miami Beach Police Department	FL	1.56	2.84
Miami Department of Police	FL	2.56	2.39

Midland Police Department	TX	2.13	1.92
Milford Police Department	CT	0.23	1.25
Milwaukee Police Department	WI	1.91	2.87
Minneapolis Police Department	MN	2.65	2.07
Mobile Police Department	AL	2.72	1.03
Modesto Police Department	CA	2.85	3.04
Monroe Police Department	LA	2.14	2.57
Montgomery Police Department	AL	1.20	0.80
Mount Vernon Police Department	NY	0.72	0.99
Muncie Police Department	IN	1.75	0.41
Naperville Police Department	IL	2.46	2.12
Nashua Police Department	NH	1.78	1.20
New Bedford Police Department	MA	1.11	1.52
New Britain Police Department	CT	1.12	1.75
New Brunswick Police Department	NJ	1.57	1.63
New Orleans Police Department	LA	1.06	2.05
New Rochelle Police Department	NY	2.16	2.71
New York City Police Department	NY	2.62	1.53
Newark Police Department	NJ	2.47	1.93
Newport Beach Police Department	CA	1.88	2.75
Newport News City Police Department	VA	2.80	2.58
Newton Police Department	MA	2.11	1.98
Niagara Falls Police Department	NY	1.49	2.12
Norfolk Police Department	VA	2.88	2.90
Norman Police Department	OK	2.33	2.21
North Bergen Township Police Department	NJ	1.63	2.08
North Las Vegas Police Department	NV	0.51	0.74
North Little Rock Police Dept.	AR	2.63	1.48
North Miami Police Dept.	FL	2.72	2.07
Norwalk Department of Police Services	CT	1.64	1.82
Oak Lawn Police Department	IL	2.32	2.04
Oak Park Police Department	IL	2.49	2.32

(Continued)

Table (*Continued*)

Oakland Police Department	CA	2.06	2.41
Ocala Police Department	FL	1.85	2.60
Oceanside Police Department	CA	2.06	2.94
Odessa Police Department	TX	2.00	1.69
Ogden City Police Department	UT	2.53	2.13
Oklahoma City Police Department	OK	1.52	1.31
Omaha Police Division	NB	1.90	2.19
Ontario Police Department	CA	1.69	2.27
Orange Police Department	CA	2.34	0.75
Orlando Police Department	FL	0.63	1.94
Overland Park Police Department	KS	1.76	2.05
Parsippany-Troy Hills Police	NJ	0.65	1.65
Pasadena Police Department	CA	2.57	2.98
Pasadena Police Department	TX	1.44	2.05
Passaic City Police Department	NJ	1.10	1.76
Pawtucket Police Department	RI	1.87	1.78
Pembroke Pines Police Department	FL	0.95	1.27
Pensacola Police Department	FL	2.15	1.84
Peoria Police Department	IL	2.67	1.78
Perth Amboy Police Department	NJ	1.98	1.49
Petersburg Police Department	VA	2.74	2.41
Philadelphia Police Department	PA	1.78	1.59
Phoenix Police Department	AZ	2.47	2.31
Pine Bluff Police Department	AR	2.13	1.99
Pittsburgh Police Department	PA	1.31	2.32
Plainfiled Police Division	NJ	2.02	2.33
Plano Police Department	TX	0.57	1.32
Plantation Police Department	FL	1.93	0.66
Pomona Police Department	CA	1.51	1.71
Pompano Beach Police Department	FL	1.76	2.43
Pontiac Police Department	MI	1.63	1.78
Port Arthur Police Department	TX	2.20	2.02

Portland Police Department	OR	2.59	2.68
Portsmouth Police Department	VA	2.01	2.63
Providence Police Department	RI	1.85	1.85
Pueblo Police Department	CO	1.42	2.13
Quincy Police Department	MA	2.42	2.56
Racine Police Department	WI	2.04	2.55
Raleigh Police Department	NC	2.13	2.88
Reading Bureau of Police	PA	1.22	2.34
Redondo Beach Police Department	CA	2.85	2.73
Reno Police Department	NV	2.26	2.44
Rialto Police Department	CA	2.02	2.84
Richardson Police Department	TX	2.52	1.39
Richmond Police Department	CA	2.44	2.92
Richmond Police Department	VA	2.57	3.13
Riverside Police Department	CA	2.72	2.68
Roanoke City Police Department	VA	1.11	2.16
Rochester Police Department	NY	2.19	1.28
Rockford Police Department	IL	0.99	1.69
Rocky Mount Police Department	NC	1.92	2.44
Sacramento Police Department	CA	2.34	2.49
Saginaw Police Department	MI	1.12	1.55
Salem Police Department	OR	1.71	2.82
Salinas Police Department	CA	2.26	2.10
Salt Lake City Police Department	UT	2.34	2.99
San Angelo Police Department	TX	1.79	1.36
San Antonio Police Department	TX	1.30	2.64
San Bernardino Police Department	CA	1.88	2.88
San Diego Police Department	CA	2.67	2.67
San Francisco Police Department	CA	2.47	2.87
San Jose Police Department	CA	1.65	2.64
San Mateo Police Department	CA	2.57	1.72
Santa Ana Police Department	CA	2.27	2.76

(*Continued*)

Table   (*Continued*)

Santa Barbara Police Department	CA	2.47	2.38
Santa Clara Police Department	CA	2.42	2.66
Santa Fe Police Department	NM	1.99	1.38
Santa Monica Police Department	CA	2.48	1.80
Santa Rosa Police Department	CA	2.57	2.82
Sarasota Police Department	FL	2.28	2.15
Savannah Police Department	GA	1.88	2.54
Schaumburg Police Department	IL	1.89	2.98
Schenectady Police Department	NY	1.60	0.80
Scottsdale Police Department	AZ	2.62	2.98
Seattle Police Department	WA	2.78	2.51
Shreveport Police Department	LA	1.97	2.07
Simi Valley Police Department	CA	1.41	0.90
Sioux City Police Department	IA	2.28	1.87
Sioux Falls Police Department	SD	1.15	2.18
Skokie Police Department	IL	1.86	2.00
Somerville Police Department	MA	0.67	1.63
South Bend Police Department	IN	1.06	2.00
Southfield Police Department	MI	2.25	1.36
Spartanburg Public Safety Department	SC	2.15	2.74
Spokane Police Department	WA	1.84	2.35
Springfield Police Department	IL	2.05	2.45
Springfield Police Department	MA	2.05	2.27
Springfield Police Department	MO	1.92	2.43
St. Joseph Police	MO	2.77	2.03
St. Louis Police Department	MO	2.57	2.64
St. Paul Police Department	MN	2.61	2.30
St. Petersburg Police Deparment	FL	2.81	2.19
Stamford Police Department	CT	1.39	1.90
Sterling Heights Police Department	MI	0.98	1.25
Stockton Police Department	CA	2.38	2.87
Sunnyvale Department of Public Safety	CA	1.55	2.37

Sunrise Police Department	FL	2.54	2.72
Syracuse Police Department	NY	1.23	2.70
Tacoma Police Department	WA	0.82	1.43
Tallahassee Police Department	FL	1.61	2.24
Tampa Police Department	FL	1.85	1.53
Taylor Police Department	MI	0.19	0.88
Tempe Police Department	AZ	2.29	2.76
Terre Haute Police Department	IN	0.99	1.12
Toledo Police Department	OH	2.28	2.59
Tonawanda Police Department	NY	1.91	1.50
Topeka Police Department	KS	1.62	2.29
Torrance Police Department	CA	1.56	2.20
Trenton Police Division	NJ	1.46	0.81
Troy Police Department	MI	2.18	2.15
Troy Police Department	NY	0.68	2.11
Tucson Police Department	AZ	1.49	3.08
Tulsa Police Department	OK	2.32	2.10
Tuscaloosa Police Department	AL	2.07	1.59
Tyler Police Department	TX	2.39	1.51
Union City Police Department	NJ	0.80	0.76
Union Department of Public Safety Police Division	NJ	1.37	1.87
Vallejo Police Department	CA	1.97	1.74
Virginia Beach Police Department	VA	1.63	2.37
Waco Police Department	TX	1.73	2.91
Waltham Police Department	MA	2.60	2.94
Warren Police Department	MI	1.14	0.43
Warwick Police Department	RI	1.66	1.28
Washington D.C. Metropolitan Police Department	DC	2.67	2.36
Waterbury Police Department	CT	1.15	1.10
Waterloo Police Department	IA	1.41	2.30
Waukegan Police Department	IL	1.62	2.45

(*Continued*)

Table   (*Continued*)

Wayne Police Department	NJ	0.96	0.86
West Allis Police Department	WI	0.87	0.92
West Covina Police Department	CA	1.86	2.24
West Haven Department of Police Services	CT	0.51	0.77
West New York Police Department	NJ	0.83	0.79
West Palm Beach Police Department	FL	2.79	2.63
West Valley Police Department	UT	1.76	1.91
Westland City Police Department	MI	1.40	0.73
Westminster Police Department	CO	2.50	2.78
White Plains Department of Public Safety	NY	1.89	2.32
Wichita Falls Police Department	TX	0.80	2.01
Wichita Police Department	KS	2.32	2.90
Wilmington Department of Police	DE	1.70	1.68
Wilmington Police Department	NC	1.20	2.05
Winston-Salem Police Department	NC	2.66	2.43
Woonsocket Police Department	RI	0.68	1.36
Worcester Police Department	MA	2.18	2.00
Yakima Police Department	WA	2.29	3.08
Yonkers Police Department	NY	1.14	1.51
Youngstown Police Dept.	OH	1.85	0.79

NOTES

Chapter 2

1. Essentially, factor analysis pools information from directly observed variables to derive a relationship to or an estimate of an unmeasured or latent construct. Confirmatory factor analysis requires that the relationships between each observed variable and latent construct be determined a priori, whereas exploratory factor analysis does not.
2. A tetrachoric correlation is one that is calculated between two dichotomous variables, and a polychoric correlation is one that is calculated between two ordinal variables.
3. Maguire and Mastrofski (2000) were testing the hypothesis that the number of dimensions diminished over time, as institutional isomorphism would suggest. Although their findings, based on 1993 Police Foundation data and 1994 to 1997 COPS Office data, appear to provide some evidence for this, they acknowledge the results are influenced by the questionnaire, sample, and method used to assess the factors, citing two unpublished studies with contradictory findings. One of these (Maguire, Zhao, and Lovrich, 1999) found that over a three-year period,

COP went from a unidimensional to multidimensional form. Another (Maguire et al., 1999) used confirmatory rather than exploratory methods to discern two rather than five dimensions of community policing in the Police Foundation data.

4. Maguire and Uchida (2000, p. 540) advise, "Measurement error is probably a significant problem in police organizational research but we cannot know for sure because researchers have, by and large, ignored it. Few police researchers have systematically accounted for measurement error in their data." The shortcomings of attempts to measure COP implementation may help account for the lack of association or unexpected relationships among various measures.

5. Lester and Goggin (1998) also sparked a debate in *Policy Currents*, the official newsletter of the Public Policy Section of the American Political Science Association, over implementation research when they typologized implementation researchers either as positive toward the field or advocating a new approach to it. See also deLeon, 1999a, Kettunen, 2000, Lester, 2000, Meier, 1999, Schneider, 1999, and Winter, 1999.

Chapter 3

1. Drawing on the work of Meyer and Rowan (1977) and Dimaggio and Powell (1983), Crank and Langworthy (1992) identified three processes by which myths are created in the institutional environment of policing. These are (1) official legitimacy from legal mandates, rules of practice, licensing, and other procedures prescribed by judicial authorities, (2) the elaboration of relational networks, or the process by which the connectedness between spheres of activity in a particular institutional environment (e.g., between police and organized labor, higher education, and the federal government), and (3) organizational-institutional reactivity where police organizations, professional associations, and leadership actively attempt to construct and shape myths in their institutional environment. Myths derived from any of these processes can influence the structure and activities of police organizations.

2. Not all organizations are equally susceptible to pressure from the institutional environment. Zucker (1987) summarized three groups of reasons why some organizations are influenced by institutional expectations more than others. First, organizations advocating unpopular values and goals are more likely to face opposition (Clark, 1956). Second, some organizations legitimate their activities by controlling or shaping the institutional environment (Dowling and Pfeffer, 1975;

Pfeffer and Salancik, 1978). Third, some organizations attempt to exert control over their boundaries and thereby mediate external influences (Thompson, 1967). The extent to which organizations can manage external influences determines their susceptibility to the influence of myths (Meyer and Zucker, 1989).

3. In a critical review of Donaldson's book, Strauss and Hanson (1997) agree that these theories are fairly exclusive and generally fail to acknowledge the contributions of others.

Chapter 4

1. Police organization size and city population are, of course, highly correlated. The relationship is such that Langworthy (1986, p. 123) contends "it is virtually impossible to disentangle the size of the served population and the size of the agency." Both variables, then, should exhibit similar influences on organizations.

2. Duncan (1972) found organizations operating in simple, stable environments to face low uncertainty, those in complex but stable environments to face low-moderate uncertainty, those in simple but unstable environments to face high-moderate uncertainty, and those in complex and unstable environments to face the highest level of uncertainty.

3. Zhao used the percentage of nonwhite residents to measure heterogeneity; percentages of families comprising married couples, householders owning their homes, persons who had graduated high school, persons who were unemployed, and persons living below the poverty line to measure socioeconomic status; and percent population change and percent of persons who lived elsewhere five years previously as measures of mobility.

Chapter 5

1. Decentralization as it pertains to police organizations is often confused with spatial differentiation (Moore and Stephens, 1991; Roberg, 1979). Although geographically dispersed organizations (e.g., those with many substations) may frequently be more decentralized, decentralization and spatial differentiation are mutually exclusive properties. The hierarchical level at which decisions are made, centralization, is not necessarily related to the extent to which the organization is spread over space, geographic dispersion.

2. Pugh et al. (1963) characterized flexibility in terms of amount, speed, and acceleration of change in organizational structure. Such a definition renders flexibility a quality of another dimension rather than an actual dimension itself.

3. Such ratios have also been called administrative weight, density, and intensity. Common ratios include the proportion of employees who are assigned administrative or support tasks.

4. Weiss (1992 and 1997) pioneered the use of these measurement techniques in the context of police innovation.

5. Damanpour included a measure of professionalism in his correlation analysis but did not include it in his multiple regressions because it was highly correlated with organization size. The correlation analysis showed professionalism to be positively related to technological innovation.

Chapter 6

1. Dewar and Hage (1978) provide some empirical support for this claim. Their data on 16 social service organizations at three time points led them to conclude that large organizations add hierarchical levels as a result of an increase in task scope. They also found task scope increases horizontal differentiation if the organization is sufficiently large and that task scope is positively associated with occupational differentiation.

2. This is a measure of what Perrow (1967) describes as task variability.

3. In another study, Maguire (1997) found no difference in civilianization, height, functional differentiation, formalization, or administrative density between police agencies that claim to practice COP and those that do not, thereby suggesting that structure may not vary with routineness of technology.

Chapter 7

1. Although the response was quite high, it is not possible to calculate exact response rates. The LEMAS survey documentation notes there are 529 "large" local police agencies, but this figure includes county and municipal organizations. This figure may also include agencies that were anticipated to have, but did not actually have, at least one hundred full-time equivalent sworn employees at the time of the survey. Excluding from the population the number of county agencies who responded, and assuming all agencies responding and all remaining agencies surveyed were of the requisite size and municipal agencies, one may calculate a

response rate of 93 percent for 1997 (462 of 499) and 99 percent for 1999 (497 of 500).

2. To improve the testing of the COP measurement model, I examined COP measures for all large police organizations available in the 1997 (n=462) and 1999 (n=497) LEMAS surveys, instead of the sample used for the structural analysis, which is smaller because of the matching process.

3. Five cases have estimated ages exceeding 167, thereby indicating they were established prior to 1830. Because the earliest modern police organizations were not established until 1838 in Boston (Lane, 1992) and 1845 in New York City (Langworthy and Travis, 1994), these observations were replaced with the mean of the variable.

4. To test Stinchcombe's (1965) hypothesis that organizations are permanently affected by the time frame in which they were established, I also constructed a dichotomous variable representing the era in which the organization was founded, either in the nineteenth century, the political era of policing, or the twentieth, comprising the reform and community problem-solving eras of policing (see Kelling and Moore, 1988). Ideally, I would have three values for this variable, with the third identifying organizations founded in the community-policing era, but there were only four such organizations. The dichotomous-era variable caused severe multicollinearity when included in the model with organization age. Because organization age somewhat captures the effect of founding era (and is important for assessing organizational experience), I excluded organizational era from the model.

5. These functions included traffic law enforcement, responding to calls for service, homicide investigation, ballistics testing, underwater recovery, traffic direction and control, accident investigations, dispatching calls for service, emergency medical services, vice enforcement, fingerprint processing, crime lab services, bomb disposal, search and rescue, school crossing services, tactical operations, parking enforcement, executing arrest warrants, court security, jail operations, serving civil process, civil defense, fire services, animal control, enforcement of drug laws, investigating violent crimes besides homicide, investigating arsons, investigating other property crimes, and investigating environmental crimes.

6. Mathematically, the Gibbs-Martin D is calculated as

$$D = 1 - \Sigma p_i^2$$

where p_i is the proportion of elements in each group. Gibbs and Martin (1962) originally developed this measure to gauge division of labor. Maguire (2003) and King (1998) also used this measure to gauge heterogeneity, as the research in this book does.

7. Thirty-seven organizations did not report their number of chiefs to Maguire; the median value of four was imputed for these.

8. Thirty-two organizations with a missing value were assigned the median (which also equals the mode because this is a dichotomous variable) value of 1.

9. Occupational differentiation is often referred to as "civilianization" and measured as the proportion of total employees that is nonsworn. There is a 0.97 correlation between this measure of civilianization and occupational differentiation in the 1997 data.

10. Thirty-eight cases were missing for this variable, for which I imputed the mean number of ranks.

11. These included bias/hate crime, child abuse, community crime prevention, community policing, crime analysis, domestic violence, drug education in schools, drunk drivers, environmental crimes, gangs, juvenile crime, missing children, police-prosecutor relations, repeat offenders, research and planning, victim assistance, and youth outreach.

12. This index was adapted from Robbins (1987). See Tables 6.5 and 6.6 in Maguire (2003) for specific information regarding these questions.

13. The alpha reliability coefficient of these 20 questions was 0.80, which suggests they are fairly good indicators of a common concept.

14. The mean value was imputed for 38 organizations with missing values.

15. These were deadly force/firearm discharge, handling the mentally ill, handling the homeless, handling domestic disputes, handling juveniles, use of less-than-lethal force, code of conduct and appearance, citizen complaints, maximum hours worked by officers, and discretionary arrest power. The 1997 LEMAS also inquired about relationships with private security firms, off-duty employment of sworn personnel, strip searches, use of confidential funds, and employee counseling assistance, but these were not asked in the 1999 LEMAS.

16. In the 1997 LEMAS, each of the four variables pertaining to administrative and technical tasks had two missing values estimated by the Census Bureau, the administrator of the survey. The Census Bureau also estimated one value for the number of full-time sworn employees and three values of the number of full-time nonsworn personnel. In 1999, the Census Bureau imputed data for seven organizations that had missing values for employees assigned to administrative and technical support tasks.

17. The specified groups were neighborhood associations, tenant associations, youth service organizations, advocacy groups, business groups, religious groups, school groups, or other groups.

18. The specified methods were in-person, telephone, Internet/webpage, public kiosk/terminal, newsletter, newspaper, radio, television, or other means.

19. I use this model to estimate COP implementation, but as with any latent construct, it is possible that the construct represents some other phenomenon (e.g., innovativeness or professionalism). Latent constructs are best defined by their measures and the theories and research from which they derive. I constructed this model based on community policing literature and therefore assume it represents COP implementation.

20. This correlation matrix contains a specific type of correlation in each cell depending on the type of variables correlated. A polychoric correlation is calculated if the two variables are ordinal or dichotomous. A polyserial correlation is calculated if one variable is continuous and the other is ordinal or dichotomous. A product-moment (Pearson) correlation is calculated if both variables are continuous.

21. Having only one endogenous variable, a classic single-equation regression model is simply a specific (reduced) form of the more general structural, path model. Because it is not hypothesized to affect itself, the B coefficient matrix is zero, which simply leaves the endogenous variable a function of the exogenous variables and the error in the equation.

Chapter 8

1. Latent constructs are estimated from directly measured variables, each of which could be measured differently, so they have no scale of their own. For a measurement model to be identified, a scale must be given to the latent construct. This is typically done by constraining the factor loading of a measure to 1, which sets the scale of the construct to that measure. See Appendix A for more information on this process.

2. Rigdon (1997) notes most structural equation experts interpret the Chi-square heuristically as it is a function of many things, such as distribution of the data and sample size. He recommends indices such as the Root Mean Square Error of Approximation (RMSEA), which relax the assumption of perfect fit in the population. There are no established "cut-offs" for statistics like RMSEA to determine which specific values constitute a good fit, though there is general agreement that values closest to a threshold (e.g., zero or one) indicate a better fitting model than those further away. As an operational guideline, I generally considered the following to indicate a reasonable fit: (1) a Normed Fit Index (NFI), Non-Normed Fit Index (NNFI) (reported for the structural model),

Incremental Fit Index (IFI), Comparative Fit Index (CFI), Goodness of Fit Index (GFI) (reported for the multi-group analyses), and Adjusted Goodness of Fit Index (AGFI) of at least 0.90; (2) an RMSEA and Standardized Root Mean Square Residual (Standardized RMR) of no more than 0.10; and (3) a nonsignificant Chi-square. Such an approach is necessary to assess fit, especially because there are so few studies that provide fit indices of similar constructs such that standard values could be created. I evaluated the evidence provided by all fit measures holistically and did not reject a model simply because a single measure (e.g., the strict Chi-square test) did not fall within these guidelines. The decision to accept a model specification rested on whether the weight of the evidence suggested a proper fitting model. See Appendix A for information regarding these fit measures.

3. For a discussion and explanation of these tests, see Bollen (1989).

Appendix A

1. It is also possible to give a latent construct a scale by setting the variance of the construct to one, thereby standardizing it. However, I followed the general practice of scaling the construct to a measure.

2. Tanaka and Huba (1984 and 1985) developed a generalized least squares version of this index.

3. This strategy is not uncommon in the context of police studies. Davenport (1996), Maguire (2003), King (1998), and Zhao, Thurman, and Lovrich (1995) offer examples of both exploratory and confirmatory factor analyses where factors related to policing are assessed either individually or within theoretically related components.

Appendix B

1. I calculated the weights by conducting a factor score regression, which regressed the COP implementation latent construct on all the directly observed COP activities in the model.

REFERENCES

Alexander, E. R. (1985). From idea to action, notes for a contingency theory of the policy implementation process. *Administration and Society, 16,* 403–26.

Anderson, J. C. and Gerbing, D. W. (1988). Structural equation modeling in practice: A review and recommended two-step approach. *Psychological Bulletin, 103,* 411–23.

Angell, J. E. (1971). Toward an alternative to the classic police organizational arrangements: A democratic model. *Criminology, 9,* 185–06.

Angell, J. E. (1975). The democratic model needs a fair trial: Angell's response. *Criminology, 12,* 379–84.

Angell, J. E. (1976). Organizing police for the future: An update of the democratic model. *Criminal Justice Review, 1,* 35–52.

Bayley, D. H. (1988). Community policing: A report from the devil's advocate. In J. R. Greene and S. D. Mastrofski (Eds.), *Community policing: Rhetoric or reality* (pp. 225–58). New York: Praeger.

Beck, K. and Wilson, C. (1997). Police officers' views on cultivating organizational commitment: Implications for police managers. *Policing: An International Journal of Police Strategy and Management, 20,* 175–95.

Bentler, P. M. (1990). Comparative fit indexes in structural models. *Psychological Bulletin, 107*, 238–46.

Bentler, P. M. and Bonett, D. G. (1980). Significance tests and goodness-of-fit in the analysis of covariance structures. *Psychological Bulletin, 88*, 588–600.

Berman, P. (1980). *Thinking about programmed and adaptive implementation: Matching strategies to situations.* Beverly Hills: Sage.

Blau, P. M. (1970). A formal theory of differentiation in organizations. *American Sociological Review, 35*, 201–18.

Blau, P. M., Heydebrand, W. V. and Stauffer, R. E. (1966). The structure of small bureaucracies. *American Sociological Review, 31*, 179–91.

Blau, P. M. and Schoenherr, R. A. (1971). *The structure of organizations.* New York: Basic Books.

Bollen, K. A. (1989). *Structural equations with latent variables.* New York: Wiley.

Browne, M. W. and Cudeck, R. (1993). Alternative ways of assessing model fit. In K. A. Bollen and J. S. Long (Eds.), *Testing Structural Equation Models* (pp. 136–62). Newbury Park, CA: Sage.

Brüderl, J. and Schüssler, R. (1990). Organizational mortality: The liabilities of newness and adolescence. *Administrative Science Quarterly, 35*, 530–47.

Bullock, C. S. III (1984). Conditions associated with policy implementation. In C. S. Bullock III and C. M. Lamb (Eds.), *Implementation of Civil Rights Policy* (pp. 184–207). Monterey, CA: Brooks/Cole Publishing.

Bureau of Justice Statistics (1999a). Law Enforcement Management and Administrative Statistics, 1997. *Bureau of Justice Statistics: Executive summary [NCJ 175712].* Washington, DC: Office of Justice Programs, U. S. Department of Justice.

Bureau of Justice Statistics. (1999b). *Law Enforcement Management and Administrative Statistics, 1997.* Conducted by the U.S. Census Bureau, edited and maintained by the Inter-university Consortium for Political and Social Research. Ann Arbor, MI.

Bureau of Justice Statistics. (2000). *Law Enforcement Management and Administrative Statistics, 1999.* Conducted by the U.S. Census Bureau, edited and maintained by the Inter-university Consortium for Political and Social Research. Ann Arbor, MI.

Burns, T. and Stalker, G. M. (1961). *The management of innovation.* London: Tavistock.

Child, J. (1972). Organization structure and strategies of control: A replication of the Aston study. *Administrative Science Quarterly, 17*, 163–77.

Child, J. (1973a). Predicting and understanding organizational structure. *Administrative Science Quarterly, 18*, 168–85.

Child, J. (1973b). Strategies of control and organizational behavior. *Administrative Science Quarterly, 18*, 1–17.

Clark, B. R. (1956). *Adult education in transition*. Berkeley: University of California Press.

COPS (2001). Data on grantees [provided per request]. Washington, DC: U.S. Department of Justice.

COPS. (2005). *Office of Community Oriented Policing Services* [online]. Available from World Wide Web: http://www.cops.usdoj.gov/Default.asp?Item=35.

Cordner, G. W. (1978). Open and closed models of police organizations: Traditions, dilemmas, and practical considerations. *Journal of Police Science and Administration, 6,* 22–34.

Cordner, G. W. (1989). Written rules and regulations: Are they necessary? *FBI Law Enforcement Bulletin, 58,* 17–21.

Crank, J. P. and Langworthy, R. H. (1992). An institutional perspective of policing. *Journal of Criminal Law and Criminology, 83,* 338–63.

Crank, J. P. (1994). Watchman and community: Myth and institutionalization in policing. *Law & Society Review, 28,* 325–51.

Daft, R. L. (1982). Bureaucratic versus nonbureaucratic structure in the process of innovation in change. In S. B. Bacharach (Ed.), *Perspectives in organizational sociology: Theory and research* (pp. 129–66). Greenwich, Conn.: JAI Press.

Daft, R. L. (2001). *Organization theory and design.* (7 ed.) Cincinnati: South-Western College Publishing.

Damanpour, F. (1987). The adoption of technological, administrative, and ancillary innovations: Impact of organizational factors. *Journal of Management, 13,* 675–88.

Damanpour, F. (1991). Organizational innovation: A meta-analysis of effects of determinants and moderators. *Academy of Management Review, 34,* 555–90.

Davenport, D. R. (1996). *Public agency performance and structure: Assessing the effects of the organizational environment.* Doctoral dissertation, Texas Tech University.

Davis, G., Muhlhausen, D. B., Ingram, D., and Rector, R. (2000). *The Facts about COPS: A Performance Overview of the Community Oriented Policing Services Program.* Report No. CDA00-10. Washington, DC: Heritage Foundation (Center for Data Analysis).

deLeon, P. (1999a). Cold comfort indeed: A rejoinder to Lester and Goggin. *Policy Currents, 8,* 6–8.

deLeon, P. (1999b). The missing link revisited: Contemporary implementation research. *Policy Studies Review, 16,* 311–38.

Dewar, R. and Hage, J. (1978). Size, technology, complexity, and structural differentiation: Toward a theoretical synthesis. *Administrative Science Quarterly, 23,* 111–36.

DiMaggio, P. J. and Powell, W. W. (1983). The iron cage revisited: Institutional isomorphism and collective rationality in organization fields. *American Sociological Review, 48*, 147–60.

Donaldson, L. (1987). Strategy and structural adjustment to regain fit and performance: In defence of contingency theory. *Journal of Management Studies, 24*, 1–24.

Donaldson, L. (1995). *American anti-management theories of organization: A critique of paradigm proliferation.* Great Britain: Cambridge University Press.

Dowling, J. and Pfeffer, J. (1975). Organizational legitimacy. *Pacific Sociological Review, 18*, 122–36.

Downs, A. (1967). *Inside bureaucracy.* Boston: Little, Brown.

Dryzek, J. S. and Ripley, B. (1988). The ambitions of policy design. *Policy Studies Review, 7*, 705–19.

Duncan, R. B. (1972). Characteristics of organizational environment and perceived environmental uncertainty. *Administrative Science Quarterly, 17*, 313–27.

Duncan, R. B. (1976). The ambidextrous organization: Designing dual structures for innovation. In R. H. Kilmann, L. R. Pondy, and D. P. Slevin (Eds.), *The Management of Organization: Strategies and Implementation* (pp. 167–88). New York: North-Holland.

Durkheim, E. (1933). *The division of labor in society.* New York: Macmillan.

Eck, J. E., and Rosenbaum, D. P. (2000). The new police order: Effectiveness, equity, and efficiency in community policing. In R. W. Glensor, M. E. Correia, and K. J. Peak (Eds.), *Policing Communities: Understanding Crime and Solving Problems* (pp. 30–45). Los Angeles, CA: Roxbury Publishing Company.

Elmore, R. F. (1985). Forward and backward mapping: Reversible logic in the analysis of public policy. In K. Hanf and T. A. J. Toonen (Eds.), *Policy Implementation in Federal and Unitary Systems* (pp. 33–70). Boston: M. Nijhoff.

Ettlie, J. E., Bridges, W. P., and O'Keefe, R. D. (1984). Organization strategy and structural differences for radical versus incremental innovation. *Management Science, 30*, 682–95.

Flanagan, T. (1985). Consumer perspectives on police organizational strategy. *Journal of Police Science and Administration, 13*, 10–21.

Gibbs, J. P. and Martin, W. T. (1962). Urbanization, technology, and the division of labor. *American Sociological Review, 27*, 667–77.

Glensor, R. W. and Peak, K. (1996). Implementing change: Community-oriented policing and problem solving. *Law Enforcement Bulletin, 65*, 14–21.

Goggin, M. L. (1986). The "too few cases/too many variables" problem in implementation research. *Western Political Quarterly, 38*, 328–47.

Goldstein, H. (1987). Toward community-oriented policing: Potential, basic requirements, and threshold questions. *Crime and Delinquency, 33*, 6–30.

Goldstein, H. (1990). *Problem-oriented policing.* New York: McGraw-Hill.

Greene, H. T. (1993). Community-oriented policing in Florida. *American Journal of Police, 12*, 141–55.

Greene, J. R. (2000). Community policing in America: Changing the nature, structure, and function of the police. In J. Horney (Ed.), *Criminal Justice 2000 (Vol. 3): Policies, Processes, and Decisions of the Criminal Justice System [NCJ 182410]* (pp. 299–370). Washington, DC: Office of Justice Programs, U.S. Department of Justice.

Greene, J. R. (1998). Evaluating planned change strategies in modern law enforcement: Implementing community-based policing. In J. Brodeur (Ed.), *How to Recognize Good Policing: Problems and Issues* (pp. 141–60). Thousand Oaks, CA: Sage.

Greene, J. R., Bergman, W. T., and McLaughlin, E. J. (1994). Implementing community policing: Cultural and structural change in police organizations. In D. P. Rosenbaum (Ed.), *The Challenge of Community Policing: Testing the Promises* (pp. 92–109). Thousand Oaks, CA: Sage.

Haarr, R. N. (1997). "They're making a bad name for the department": Exploring the link between organizational commitment and police occupational deviance in a police patrol bureau. *Policing: An International Journal of Police Strategy and Management, 20*, 786–812.

Hage, J. (1965). An axiomatic theory of organizations. *Administrative Science Quarterly, 10*, 289–320.

Hage, J. and Aiken, M. (1967). Relationship of centralization to other structural properties. *Administrative Science Quarterly, 12*, 72–92.

Hall, R. H. (1968). Professionalization and bureaucratization. *American Sociological Review, 33*, 92–104.

Hall, R. H. (1972). *Organizations: Structure and process.* Englewood Cliffs: Prentice-Hall.

Hall, R. H., Johnson, N. J., and Haas, J. E. (1967). Organizational size, complexity, and formalization. *Administrative Science Quarterly, 32*, 903–12.

Harvey, E. (1968). Technology and the structure of organizations. *American Sociological Review, 33*, 247–59.

Henderson, T. A. (1975). The relative effects of community complexity and of sheriffs upon the professionalism of sheriff departments. *American Journal of Political Science, 19*, 107–32.

Hickman, M. J. and Reaves, B. A. (2001). Community policing in local police departments, 1997 and 1999. *Bureau of Justice Statistics: Special report [NCJ 184794].* Washington, DC: Office of Justice Programs, U. S. Department of Justice.

Hirsch, P. M. (1975). Organizational effectiveness and the institutional environment. *Administrative Science Quarterly, 20,* 327–44.

Hsu, C. K., Marsh, R. M., and Mannari, H. (1983). An examination of the structural determinants of organizational structure. *American Journal of Sociology, 88,* 975–96.

Joreskog, K. and Sorbom, D. (1986). *LISREL VI: Analysis of linear structural relationships by maximum likelihood and least squares methods.* Mooresville, IN: Scientific Software International, Inc.

Joreskog, K. and Sorbom, D. (1996). *LISREL 8: User's reference guide.* Chicago: Scientific Software International, Inc.

Kaplan, D. (2000). *Structural equation modeling: Foundations and extensions.* Thousand Oaks, CA: Sage.

Katz, D. and Kahn, R. L. (1966). *The social psychology of organizations.* New York: Wiley.

Kelling, G. L., Pate, A., Ferrara, A., Utne, M., and Brown, C. E. (1981). *Newark foot patrol experiment.* Washington, DC: Police Foundation.

Kelling, G. L. and Moore, M. H. (1988). The evolving strategy of policing. *Perspectives on policing* (Vol. 4). Washington, DC: National Institute of Justice, U.S. Department of Justice.

Kelling, G. L. and Coles, C. M. (1996). *Fixing broken windows: Restoring order & reducing crime in our communities.* New York: The Free Press.

Kelman, S. (1984). Using implementation research to solve implementation problems: The case of energy emergency assistance. *Journal of Policy Analysis and Management, 4,* 75–91.

Kettunen, P. (2000). Implementation approach: The political scientists' perspective. *Policy Currents, 10,* 3–5.

Kimberly, J. R. (1976). Organizational size and the structuralist perspective: A review, critique, and proposal. *Administrative Science Quarterly, 21,* 571–97.

King, W. R. (1998). *Innovativeness in American municipal police organizations.* Doctoral dissertation, University of Cincinnati.

King, W. R. (1999). Time, constancy, and change in American municipal police organizations. *Police Quarterly, 2,* 338–64.

King, W. R. (2000). Measuring police innovation: Issues and measurement. *Policing: An International Journal of Police Strategy and Management, 23,* 303–17.

Kuykendall, J. and Roberg, R. R. (1982). Mapping police organizational change: From a mechanistic to an organic model. *Criminology, 20,* 241–56.

Lane, R. (1992). Urban police and crime in nineteenth century America. In M. Tonry and N. Morris (Eds.), *Modern Policing* (pp. 1–50). Chicago: University of Chicago Press.

Langworthy, R. H. (1986). *The structure of police organizations.* New York: Praeger.

Langworthy, R. H. and Travis, L. F. (1994). *Policing in America: A balance of forces.* New York: Macmillan.

Lawrence, P. R. and Lorsch, J. W. (1967). *Organization and environment.* Boston: Harvard University.

Lester, J. P. (2000). Back to the future in implementation research: A response. *Policy Currents, 10,* 2–3.

Lester, J. P., Bowman, A. O., Goggin, M. L., and O'Toole, L. J. Jr. (1987). Public policy implementation: Evolution of the field and agenda for future research. *Policy Studies Review, 7,* 200–16.

Lester, J. P. and Goggin, M. L. (1998). Back to the future: The rediscovery of implementation studies. *Policy Currents, 8,* 1–9.

Levinthal, D. A. and Fichman, M. (1988). Dynamics of interorganizational attachments: Auditor-client relationships. *Administrative Science Quarterly, 33,* 345–69.

Linder, S. H. and Peters, B. G. (1987). A design perspective on policy implementation: The fallacies of misplaced prescription. *Policy Studies Review, 6,* 459–76.

MacCallum, R. C., Wegener, D. T., Uchino, B. N., and Fabrigar, L. R. (1993). The problem of equivalent models in applications of covariance structure analysis. *Psychological Bulletin, 114,* 185–99.

Maguire, E. R. (2003). *Organizational structure in American police agencies: Context, complexity, and control.* Albany, NY: SUNY Press.

Maguire, E. R. (1997). Structural change in large municipal police organizations during the community policing era. *Justice Quarterly, 14,* 547–76.

Maguire, E. R. and Katz, C. M. (2002). Community policing, loose coupling, and sensemaking in American police agencies. *Justice Quarterly, 19,* 503–36.

Maguire, E. R., Kuhns, J. B., Uchida, C. D., and Cox, S. M. (1997). Patterns of community policing in nonurban America. *Journal of Research in Crime and Delinquency, 34,* 368–94.

Maguire, E. R. and Mastrofski, S. D. (2000). Patterns of community policing in the United States. *Police Quarterly, 3,* 4–45.

Maguire, E. R. and Uchida, C. D. (2000). Measurement and explanation in the comparative study of American police organizations. In D. Duffee (Ed.), *Criminal justice 2000 (Vol. 4): Measurement and analysis of crime and justice [NCJ 182411]* (pp. 491–557). Washington, DC: Office of Justice Programs, U.S. Department of Justice.

Maguire, E. R., Uchida, C. D., Kuhns, J. B., and Cox, S. M. (1999). *Measuring community policing at the agency level.* Unpublished manuscript.

Maguire, E. R., Zhao, J., and Lovrich, N. (1999). *Dimensions of community policing.* Unpublished manuscript.

Maslow, A. H. (1943). A theory of human motivation. *Psychological Review, 50,* 370–96.

Mastrofski, S. D. (1998). Community policing and police organization structure. In J. Brodeur (Ed.), *How to recognize good policing: Problems and issues* (pp. 161–240). Thousand Oaks, CA: Sage.

Matland, R. E. (1995). Synthesizing the implementation literature: The ambiguity-conflict model of policy implementation. *Journal of Public Administration Research and Theory, 5,* 145–74.

McCabe, K. A. and Fajardo, R. G. (2001). Law enforcement accreditation: A national comparison of accredited vs. nonaccredited agencies. *Journal of Criminal Justice, 29,* 127–31.

Meier, K. J. (1999). Are we sure Lasswell did it this way? Lester, Goggin and implementation research. *Policy Currents, 9,* 5–8.

Meyer, M. W. (1990). Notes of a skeptic: from organizational ecology to organizational evolution. In J. V. Singh (Ed.) *Organizational evolution: New directions* (pp. 298–314). Newbury Park, CA: Sage.

Meyer, M. W. (1972). Size and structure of organizations: A causal analysis. *American Sociological Review, 37,* 434–40.

Meyer, M. W. and Brown, M. C. (1977). The process of bureaucratization. *American Journal of Sociology, 83,* 364–85.

Meyer, J. W. and Rowan, B. (1977). Institutionalized organizations: Formal structure as myth and ceremony. *American Journal of Sociology, 83,* 340–63.

Meyer, J. W. and Scott, W. R. (1983). *Organizational environments: Ritual and rationality.* Beverly Hills: Sage Publications.

Meyer, M. W. and Zucker, L. G. (1989). *Permanently failing organizations.* Newbury Park, CA: Sage Publications.

Moore, M. H. (1992). Problem solving and community policing. In M. Tonry and N. Morris (Eds.), *Modern policing* (pp. 99–158). Chicago: University of Chicago Press.

Moore, M. H. and Stephens, D. W. (1991). *Beyond command and control: The strategic management of police organizations.* Washington, DC: Police Executive Research Forum.

Morgan, G. (1997). *Images of organizations* (2nd ed.). Thousand Oaks, CA:Sage.

Muhlhausen, D. B. (2001). *Do community oriented policing services grants affect violent crime rate?* Report No. CDA01-15. Washington, DC: Heritage Foundation (Center for Data Analysis).

Ostrom, E. (1979). *Decision-related research on the organization of service delivery systems in metropolitan areas: Police protection*. Ann Arbor: University of Michigan.

O'Toole, L., Jr. (1986). Policy recommendations for multi-actor implementation: An assessment of the field. *Journal of Public Policy, 6,* 181–210.

O'Toole, L. J., Jr. (2000). Research on policy implementation: Assessment and prospects. *Journal of Public Administration Research and Theory, 10,* 263–88.

Palumbo, D. J. (1987). Symposium: Implementation: What have we learned and still need to know? Introduction. *Policy Studies Review, 7,* 91–102.

Parsons, T. (1961). Suggestions for a sociological approach to the theory of organizations. In A. Etzioni (Ed.), *Complex organizations: A sociological reader* (pp. 32–47). New York: Holt, Rinehart and Winston.

Perrow, C. (1967). A framework for the comparative analysis of organizations. *American Sociological Review, 32,* 194–208.

Pfeffer, J. and Salancik, G. (1978). *The external control of organizations.* New York: Harper & Row.

Pfeffer, J. (1993). Barriers to the advance of organizational science: Paradigm development as a dependent variable. *Academy of Management Review, 18,* 599–620.

Pressman, J. L. and Wildavsky, A. B. (1973). *Implementation.* Berkeley: University of California Press.

Pugh, D. S., Hickson, D. J., Hinings, C. R., and Turner, C. (1968). Dimensions of organizational structure. *Administrative Science Quarterly, 13,* 65–91.

Pugh, D. S., Hickson, D. J., Hinings, C. R., Macdonald, K. M., Turner, C., and Lupton, T. (1963). A conceptual scheme for organizational analysis. *Administrative Science Quarterly, 8,* 289–315.

Rainey, H. G. (1991). *Understanding and managing public organizations.* San Francisco: Jossey-Bass Publishers.

Ranger-Moore, J. (1997). Bigger may be better, but is older wiser? Organizational age and size in the New York life insurance industry. *American Sociological Review, 62,* 903–20.

Riechers, L. M. and Roberg, R. R. (1990). Community policing: A critical review of underlying assumptions. *Journal of Police Science and Administration, 17,* 105–14.

Rigdon, E. E. (1995). A necessary and sufficient identification rule for structural models estimated in practice. *Multivariate Behavioral Research, 30,* 359–83.

Rigdon, E. (1997, May 27). *SEMNET Discussion List* [online]. Available from World Wide Web: http://bama.ua.edu/archives/semnet.html.

Riley, K. J., Turner, S., MacDonald, J., Ridgeway, G., Schell, T., Wilson, J. M., Dixon, T., Fain, T., Barnes-Proby, D., and Fulton, B. (2005). *Police-community relations in Cincinnati.* Santa Monica, CA: RAND, TR-333-CC.

Ripley, R. B. and Franklin, G. H. (1982). *Bureaucracy and policy implementation.* Homewood, IL: Dorsey Press.

Robbins, S. P. (1987). *Organization theory: Structure, design, and applications* (2nd ed.). Englewood Cliffs, NJ: Prentice Hall.

Roberg, R. R. (1979). *Police management and organizational behavior: A contingency approach.* St. Paul, MN: West Publishing Company.

Roberg, R. R. (1994). Can today's police organizations effectively implement community policing? In D. P. Rosenbaum (Ed.), *The challenge of community policing: Testing the promises* (pp. 249–57). Thousand Oaks, CA: Sage.

Rushing, W. A. (1967). The effects of industry size and division of labor on administration. *Administrative Science Quarterly, 12,* 273–95.

Rushing, W. A. (1976). Profit and nonprofit orientations and the differentiation-coordination hypothesis for organizations: A study of small general hospitals. *American Sociological Review, 41,* 676–91.

Sadd, S. and Grinc, R. M. (1996). Implementation challenges in community policing: Innovative neighborhood-oriented policing in eight cities. *Research in brief [NCJ 157932].* Washington, DC: National Institute of Justice, U.S. Department of Justice.

Salamon, L. (1981). Rethinking public management: Third-party government and the changing forms of government action. *Public Policy, 29,* 255–275.

Schneider, A. L. (1999). Terminator! Who, me? Some thoughts about the study of policy implementation. *Policy Currents, 9,* 1–5.

Shaw, C. R. and McKay, H. D. (1972). *Juvenile delinquency and urban areas* (3rd ed.). Chicago: University of Chicago Press.

Skogan, W. G. and Hartnett, S. M. (1997). *Community policing, Chicago style.* New York: Oxford University Press.

Skolnick, J. H. and Bayley, D. (1988). Theme and variation in community policing. In M. Tonry and N. Morris (Eds.), *Crime and Justice: A Review of Research* (Vol. 10, pp. 1–37). Chicago: University of Chicago Press.

Skolnick, J. H. and Bayley, D. H. (1986). *The new blue line: Police innovation in six American cities.* New York: The Free Press.

Sorel, G. (1916). *Reflections of violence.* London: Allen & Unwin.

Sparrow, M. K. (1988). Implementing community policing. *Perspectives on Policing* (Vol. 9). Washington, DC, National Institute of Justice, U.S. Department of Justice.

Steiger, J. H. and Lind, J. M. (1980). *Statistically based tests for the number of common factors.* Paper presented at the annual meeting of the Psychometric Society, Iowa City, IA.

Steiger, J. H. (1990). Structural model evaluation and modification: An interval estimation approach. *Multivariate Behavioral Research, 25,* 173–80.

Stinchcombe, A. (1965). Social structure and organizations. In J. G. March (Ed.), *Handbook of Organizations* (pp. 142–93). Chicago: Rand McNally.

Strauss, G. and Hanson, M. (1997). Review of the book *American anti-management theories of organization: A critique of paradigm proliferation. Human Relations, 50,* 1177–90.

Strenski, I. (1987). *Four theories of myth in twentieth-century history.* Iowa City: University of Iowa Press.

Tafoya, W. L. (1997). The current state and future of community policing. *Crime & Justice International, 13,* 7–14.

Tanaka, J. S. and Huba, G. J. (1984). Confirmatory hierarchical factor analyses of psychological distress measures. *Journal of Personality and Social Psychology, 46,* 621–35.

Tanaka, J. S. and Huba, G. J. (1985). A fit index for covariance structure models under arbitrary GLS estimation. *British Journal of Mathematical and Statistical Psychology, 38,* 197–201.

Thompson, J. D. (1967). *Organizations in action.* New York: McGraw Hill.

Trojanowicz, R. (1982). *An evaluation of the neighborhood foot patrol program in Flint, Michigan.* East Lansing, MI: Michigan State University.

Trojanowicz, R. and Bucqueroux, B. (1998). *Community policing: How to get started* (2nd ed.). Cincinnati: Anderson Publishing.

Trojanowicz, R., Kappeler, V. E., Gaines, L. K., and Bucqueroux, B. (1998). *Community policing: A contemporary perspective* (2nd ed.). Cincinnati, OH: Anderson Publishing.

Tucker, L. R. and Lewis, C. (1973). A reliability coefficient for maximum likelihood factor analysis. *Psychometrika, 38,* 1–10.

Weber, M. (1946). *Essays in sociology.* New York: Oxford University Press.

Weisel, D. L. and Eck, J. E. (1994). Toward a practical approach to organizational change: Community policing initiatives in six cities. In D. P. Rosenbaum (Ed.), *The Challenge of Community Policing: Testing the Promises* (pp. 53–72). Thousand Oaks, CA: Sage.

Weiss, A. (1992). *The innovation process in public organizations: Patterns of diffusion and adoption in American policing.* Doctoral dissertation, Northwestern University.

Weiss, A. (1997). The communication of innovation in American policing. *Policing: An International Journal of Police Strategy and Management, 20,* 292–310.

Wilkinson, D. L. and Rosenbaum, D. P. (1994). The effects of organizational structure on community policing: A comparison of two cities. In D. P. Rosenbaum (Ed.), *The Challenge of Community Policing: Testing the Promises* (pp. 110–26). Thousand Oaks, CA: Sage.

Williams, W. (1976). Implementation analysis and assessment. *Policy Analysis, 1,* 531–66.

Wilson, J. M. (2003). Measurement and association in the structure of municipal police organizations. *Policing: An International Journal of Police Strategies and Management, 26,* 276–97.

Wilson, J. M. and Donnermeyer, J. F. (2002). *Problem-solving teams in the Columbus Division of Police: A final report.* Columbus, OH: Franklin County Justice Programs Unit, Office of Criminal Justice Services.

Wilson, J. Q. (1966). Innovation in organization: Notes toward a theory. In J. D. Thompson (Ed.), *Approaches to Organizational Design* (pp. 194–218). Pittsburgh, PA: University of Pittsburgh Press.

Wilson, J. Q. (1968). *Varieties of police behavior: The management of law and order in eight communities.* Cambridge: Harvard University Press.

Wilson, J. Q. and Kelling, G. L. (1982). Broken Windows: The police and neighborhood safety. *Atlantic Monthly, 249,* 29–38.

Winter, S. (1999). New directions for implementation research. *Policy Currents, 8,* 1–5.

Woodward, J. (1965). *Industrial organization: Theory and practice.* New York: Oxford University Press.

Yin, R. K. (1982). Studying the implementation of public programs. In W. Williams et al. (Eds.), *Studying implementation: Methodological and administrative issues* (pp. 36–72). Chatham, NJ: Chatham House.

Zhao, J. (1994). *Contemporary organizational change in community-oriented policing: A contingency approach.* Doctoral dissertation, Washington State University.

Zhao, J. (1996). *Why police organizations change: A study of community-oriented policing.* Washington, D.C.: Police Executive Research Forum.

Zhao, J., Thurman, Q. C., and Lovrich, N. P. (1995). Community-oriented policing across the U.S.: Facilitators and impediments to implementation. *American Journal of Police, 1,* 11–28.

Zhao, J. S., Scheider, M. C., Thurman, Q. (2002). Funding community policing to reduce crime: Have COPS grants made a difference? *Criminology & Public Policy, 2,* 7–32.

Zucker, L. G. (1987). Institutional theories of organization. *Annual Review of Sociology, 13,* 443–64.

INDEX

A

Adjusted Goodness of Fit Index
(AGFI), 77–80, 115, 117–118
Administrative weight
and COP implementation, 88
measures of, 64
and organizational context, 95–97
and organizational structure, 38–39,
42
and organization size, 48
and structural complexity, 97–98, 105
Asymptotic covariance matrix, 71, 114
Aurora (Illinois) police agency, 40
Authority, hierarchy of, 36

B

Bentler-Bonett Index, 116

C

Centralization, 36, 37–39, 40–42
and COP implementation, 88, 103
index of, 63–64
and innovation, 45
Change, measures of, 43
Chi-square test, 71, 77–80, 115, 116,
118
Citizen interaction, measures of, 66, 67,
75–77, 106
Citizen training, activity scores, 123,
125
City size, and COP implementation,
28–29
Civilianization, of police organizations,
41, 42, 48
Civilian review board, 62
Civil service employees, police as, 32